Capital Punishment:
The Inevitability
of Caprice and Mistake

CHARLES L. BLACK Jr.

Capital Punishment:
The Inevitability
of Caprice and Mistake

W·W·NORTON & COMPANY INC·

NEW YORK

To My Brother
Thomas Bowman Black

Contents

Preface

MY THANKS are due and gladly given to George Brockway, Calvin Towle, and the staff of W. W. Norton & Company; to Eileen M. Quinn and Carolyn B. Vitale, for help that transcended the secretarial; to Robert S. Davis, Yale Law School 1974, who put thought as well as research work into the product; to Dean William P. Cunningham, the University of Maryland Law School, and the Maryland Law Review, for the stimulus given me, in their invitation to deliver the Morris Ames Soper Lecture in 1972, to begin structuring my thought about this subject; to Professor Aaron Schreiber, who led me back to a half-remembered Talmudic reference; to my son Gavin B. Black, who read and helpfully commented on the manuscript; and to Barbara A. Black, with whom I have talked much on these matters. I ought also to say, though I cannot trace the exact line of indebtedness, that my thoughts on discretion and mistake owe much to the work, and to the conversation in years past, of Professor Ronald Dworkin. I also owe a general indebtedness to Professor Guido Calabresi, to Professor Jay Katz, M.D., and to Edward W. Allen, M.D., with all of whom I have so thoroughly traveled over the subject of the penalty of death. My particular debt to Dean Abraham Goldstein is specifically acknowledged in Chapter 6; my whole debt to him is more general. None of these of course is responsible for anything, except as one is necessarily responsible for the ideas one stimulates in the minds of one's friends.

C. L. B., Jr.

Chapter 1

Introduction

ALTHOUGH quite different and (to the public taste) more sensationally absorbing events have eclipsed the fact, this country is now in the midst of a great moral crisis, a crisis concerning the punishment of death. Though I oppose the death penalty on many grounds, this book deals with just two aspects of the death-penalty problem—the possibility of *mistake* in the infliction of this penalty and the presence of standardless *arbitrariness* in its infliction. I shall try to show that these two facets of the problem are in some sense the same or, at least, that they are so indissolubly connected as often to be indistinguishable. Though I hope some enlightenment may be a by-product, my aim is to persuade you that these two problems—mistake and arbitrariness in death-penalty cases—are not fringe-problems, susceptible to being mopped up by minor refinements in concept and technique, but are at the very heart of the matter and are insoluble by any methods now known or now foreseeable. If we resume use of the death penalty, we will be killing some people by mistake and some without application of comprehensible standards, and we will go on doing these things until we give up the death penalty.

Let me first sketch the immediate background, hardly old enough to be called history. Until 1967 most American states, and the federal government, occasionally inflicted the penalty of death—by hanging, by electrocution, by gas, or by shooting—for a small number of offenses, chiefly murder, but with rape an important addition in some states, and with a few other offenses included here and there. I say "occasionally" because, in the half-dozen or so years preceding 1967, the penalty of death was actually inflicted, in America, on an average of some twenty-four persons annually, out of a very much larger number who had committed offenses for which death was a possible penalty. Of those actually convicted of such offenses, the large majority escaped, through jury discretion or through clemency—the latter exercised either by state governors or by special boards set up by the law of the particular state. It is quite certain, though in the nature of the case not formally provable, that another large group of persons, who could have been convicted of capital offenses, escaped, either through being charged with a lesser and noncapital offense, or through a jury finding of "guilty" only of the "lesser included offense"—a finding probably quite often motivated by the jury's desire to prevent infliction of the death penalty. (In case this is puzzling, let me give it more concreteness. A defendant who might have been found, on the evidence, to have killed with "malice"—a most problematic term, not clarified by centuries of verbal tossing about—and so to be guilty of "murder," might be allowed by the prosecutor to plead guilty to, say, "manslaughter"—roughly, for this purpose, killing without "malice"—receiving a sentence of a term of years; or a jury, even in the face of enough evidence to support a verdict of "premeditated murder," might nevertheless find the defendant guilty only of "manslaughter," so that the greatest possible punishment was imprisonment. This is permissible, and the term "lesser included offense" is used, because killing *without* "malice" (manslaughter) can be looked on as "included" within the offense of killing *with* "malice" (murder), being composed of all the elements of the more serious offense *except* "malice," so that in proving a case of "murder" *except* for the "malice," one will have proved "manslaughter.") Since defendants escaping death in this way are never formally identified as guilty of the capital offense, it is impossible to give numbers or percentages, but no person experienced in the field doubts that the processes I have here described have very often taken place.

By 1967, a great litigation effort was well under way, aimed at persuading the Supreme Court of the United States that the infliction of death by law violated the national Constitution—in particular the Eighth Amendment, which forbids the infliction of "cruel and unusual punishments." This and various connected questions were before the Court for a long time; meanwhile, executions were "stayed" by court order, pending outcome of the suits. No person has been executed since 1967, partly because of these stays, and partly because of stays incident to now (1974) current litigation.

In June of 1972, the Supreme Court, by a five-to-four decision in the case of Furman v. Georgia, in some sense upheld the position of those attacking capital punishment. I have to say "in some sense" because *nine* full opinions were delivered, and the opinions of the five

Justices constituting the majority were not in agreement on the reasons for the decision or, by inference, on its scope as a precedent for the future. Two Justices in the majority of five would have held capital punishment to be wholly forbidden by the Constitution, as a "cruel and unusual" punishment in itself. The other three, with some variation in reasons and in expression, seemed to be holding that capital punishment *as currently administered* violated the Constitution, because of the arbitrary selection of a small number of sufferers—a selection mostly made not on clearly articulated grounds but on the basis of a standardless "discretion" lodged in juries and judges.

It would be a task of great complexity, probably not ultimately eventuating in a clear picture, to try to analyze all these opinions or to place their reasonings into harmony with other quite recent Supreme Court case-law developed by the capital punishment litigation. For purposes of the present historical sketch, it would seem to be enough to say that the decisive ground of the 1972 Furman case's anti-capital punishment ruling—the ground persuasive to the marginal Justices needed for a majority—was that, out of a large number of persons "eligible" in law for the punishment of death, a few were selected as if at random, by no stated (or perhaps statable) criteria, while all the rest suffered the lesser penalty of imprisonment.

Through the operation of causes which those of us who oppose capital punishment can only guess at, the country did not sigh with relief at the Court's having taken on itself the burden of eliminating this vestigial cruelty, bringing the United States into line with most civilized nations. Instead, a good many of the state legislatures went zealously to work, drafting and passing statutes which, it was hoped, would get around the Supreme Court decision and make it possible once more to inflict the death penalty. These statutes—and pending bills— approach this work in two principal ways. Either the death penalty is made "mandatory" for certain offenses, or there is promulgated a set of what purport to be "standards" for guidance of the selection (usually by juries) of those who are to die.

New litigation is now in progress challenging the constitutionality of these statutes. The focus of this book will not be on constitutional questions as such, but on the standardlessness and mistake-proneness of the process by which people are chosen to die, even after the passage of these new laws, and on the unacceptability of this system to us as citizens, quite apart from the question of its constitutional vulnerability.

Chapter **2**

Mistake and Arbitrariness—An Overview

I HAVE SAID that the central thesis of this book is that the problems of mistake and caprice are ineradicable in the administration of the death penalty. In a narrow sense, then, I am saying that these seemingly more "precise" statutes, just referred to, do not cure the fundamental defect that was the basis of the Supreme Court's 1972 decision in the Furman case, outlawing capital punishment as it has been administered. Though the truth of this assertion can be established from the new statutes alone (see Chapter 7), I want to make my case in a wider frame of reference. This widening will consist in opening to the reader's view the entire *series of decisions* made by the legal system as a person goes the road from freedom to the electric chair. Let us take an overview of these.

I will skip over the preliminary decision on arrest, and go on to the two-pronged decision made by the prosecutor. On the facts before him, he must first decide whether to *charge* an offense carrying the penalty of death, or a lesser offense. If he decides to charge the capital offense, he must quite commonly decide whether to *accept a plea of guilty* to a lesser (and therefore noncapital) offense, thus permitting the defendant to escape at this early stage the possibility of execution, at the price of going to prison without trial. (Now it is quite true that a grand jury often plays a part in the making of the first of these decisions—the decision on what to charge—but grand juries are commonly quite heavily under the influence of the prosecutor; in any case, the decision as to the nature of the charge brought must be made by somebody, and it will be immaterial to any of the discussion in the rest of this book whether this decision be made by the prosecutor alone or by the prosecutor in co-action with a grand jury. For this reason, and for simplicity's sake, I will from now on refer to this choice as one made by the prosecutor.)

If the *prosecutor,* having charged a capital crime, is nevertheless willing to accept a plea of guilty to a lesser offense, then the *defendant* has in turn the choice of accepting or rejecting this offer. This dreadful choice has to be made by a man in custody, often disoriented and frightened, and hence dependent upon advice, and susceptible to following possibly bad advice; at this point, then, the choice is partly or wholly made by the *lawyer* for the defendant. With the best of intentions, this lawyer's decision is often a difficult one. (The "plea bargain" will be more fully explained in Chapter 5.)

If a "plea bargain" is not struck, then the defendant goes on trial for his life. At the end of this trial, the jury has a number of decisions or choices to make, most of them

veiled by the secrecy of the jury-room. It must decide
what the gross *physical* facts were: Did this defendant, for
example, actually stab the deceased, or did somebody else
do it? Did the defendant stab the victim at a time when the
victim was trying to stab the defendant, or did he stab a
man whose knife was sheathed? (I will now mention, not
for the last time, that "mistake" as to these questions of
physical fact seems to be what most people mean when
they speak of "mistake" in criminal proceedings; I hope I
shall be able to convince you that the range of possible
"mistake" is much broader than that.) Having satisfied its
mind as to the *physical* facts, the jury must then tackle the
psychological facts. Did the defendant, who clearly (or
admittedly) shot a man while that man was reaching for
his handkerchief, *believe* that that man was reaching for a
gun, or is the pretense that he so believed mere sham? Did
the defendant *plan* this killing, or was it done in the heat
of passion? Did he *intend* to kill at all?

The jury in a criminal case does not announce its
decision on each of such points one by one. It simply
comes in with a verdict of "not guilty," or "guilty of
murder in the first degree," or of "manslaughter," or of
some other offense known to the state's law. There is no
question in the mind of anybody who has dealt with the
criminal-law system that a jury sometimes comes in with a
verdict of "guilty" of some offense lesser than the one
strictly warranted by the evidence. All kinds of factors—
sympathy, doubt of physical "guilt" in the narrow sense,
doubt as to the other, less tangible factors going to make
up "guilt," a feeling that extenuating circumstances exist,
and so on—may motivate this behavior. But the
pragmatic fact, visible from the outside, is that the jury, in
finding a defendant guilty, let us say, of "second-degree"
rather than of "first-degree" murder, is, for whatever

reason and on whatever basis, *choosing* that this defendant not suffer death.

Very commonly, at this stage, the jury must rule on the "insanity defense." I single it out for special emphasis because it is so crucially important, particularly in cases of a revolting sort, likely to inflame a jury, and also because it plumbs the whole theory of criminal responsibility. A verdict of "not guilty by reason of insanity" is a jury's choice for some form of imprisonment rather than for death. (At two other points "sanity" is a critical issue. Before the trial, a court may have to decide whether a defendant is sane enough, at that time, to be tried, and, at least theoretically, it must be decided, at the time of execution, that the defendant is sane enough to be executed (a quite puzzling concept); but the sanity question of greatest importance, by far, is the question of sanity that goes to the issue of guilt of the charged crime—sanity, that is, at the time the act was committed.)

If the jury, accepting the prosecutor's version of the facts and rejecting all defenses, convicts the defendant of an offense for which the death penalty is possible, the choice then has to be made as to *sentencing*. Under the old system, condemned in the 1972 Furman case, the usual procedure was for the jury, "in its discretion," to decide whether a death sentence was to be imposed. The form of words varied from state to state; sometimes the death sentence followed automatically unless the jury recommended mercy, while sometimes the affirmative recommendation of the jury was necessary for the sentence of death. Sometimes, indeed, the judge rather than the jury exercised this "discretion." In the newer statutes referred to in Chapter 1 (the statutes designed to get around the 1972 Furman case) a *second* hearing on sentencing often occurs, at the end of which, on the basis of mitigating or aggravating circumstances named in the new law, the sentence of death may or may not be imposed. In this initial survey, it is enough to note that this choice must usually be made. (Sometimes the sentence of death is "mandatory" on conviction of certain crimes—but note, above, that prosecutor and jury practically always retain control (by discretion in charging and in accepting a "plea," and by finding the defendant guilty of a less-than-capital offense) over the decision whether conviction of this "mandatorily" capital crime can occur.)

After conviction, sentencing, and appeal, we reach the possibility of executive clemency, or clemency exercised by a pardon board. In no state, as far as I know, is it the case that a death sentence, once imposed, *must* be carried out, without the possibility of there intervening an act of mercy by some authority. The national Constitution fixes this principle for federal crime, by giving the pardoning power to the President.

Now that is about the range, though some minor points may have been skipped, for later filling in. It becomes plainly visible that the choice of death as the penalty is the result not of just *one* choice—that of the trial judge or jury, dealt with in the Furman case—but of a *number* of choices, starting with the prosecutor's choice of a charge, and ending with the choice of the authority—the governor or a board—charged with the administration of clemency.

Regarding *each* of these choices, through all the range, one of two things, or perhaps both, may be true.

First, the choice made may be a *mistaken* one. The defendant may not have committed the act of which he is found guilty; the factors which ought properly to induce a prosecutor to accept a plea to a lesser offense may have been present, though he refused to do so; the defendant may have been "insane" in the way the law requires for exculpation, though the jury found that he was not. And so on.

Secondly, there may either be no legal standards governing the making of the choice, or the standards verbally set up by the legal system for the making of the choice may be so vague, at least in part of their range, as to be only *apparent* standards, in truth furnishing no direction and leaving the actual choice quite arbitrary.

These two possibilities have an interesting (and, in the circumstances, tragic) relationship. The concept of *mistake* fades out as the *standard* grows more and more vague and unintelligible. There is no vagueness problem about the question "Did Y hit Z on the head with a piece of pipe?" It is, for just that reason, easily possible to conceive of what it means to be "mistaken" in answering this question; one is "mistaken" if one answers it "yes" when in fact Y did not hit Z with the pipe. It is even fairly clear what it means to be "mistaken" in answering the question "Did Y *intend* to kill Z?" Conscious intents are facts; the difference here really is that, for obvious reasons, *mistake is more likely* in the second case than in the first, for it is hard or impossible to be confident of coming down on the right side of a question about past psychological fact.

It is very different when one comes to the question, "Was the action of which the defendant was found guilty performed in such a manner as to evidence an 'abandoned and malignant heart'?" (This phrase figures importantly in homicide law.) This question has the same grammatical form as a clearcut factual question; actually, through a considerable part of its range, it is not at all clear what it means. It sets up, in this range, not a standard but a *pseudo-standard*. One cannot, strictly speaking, be *mistaken* in answering it, at least within a considerable range, because to be mistaken is to be on the wrong side of a line, and there is no real line here. But that, in turn, means that the "test" may often be no test at all, but merely an invitation to arbitrariness and passion, or even to the influence of dark unconscious factors.

"Mistake" and "arbitrariness" therefore are reciprocally related. As a purported "test" becomes less and less intelligible, and hence more and more a cloak for arbitrariness, "mistake" becomes less and less possible— not, let it be strongly emphasized, because of any certainty of one's being right, but for the exactly contrary reason that there is no "right" or "wrong" discernible.

Sometimes, there is a puzzling intermediate or hybrid case, where the "test," though expressed in exceedingly obscure language, may, in some metaphysical sense, have "meaning," so that one can, in theory, be right or wrong in some application of it. But so obscurely expressed a standard *invites* mistake, even if the standard itself, in some ideal sense, is meaningful. The truth is that we mortals cannot really tell whether such obscurely expressed standards have, in some arcane sense, any meaning, so we don't know whether, in trying to apply them, we are behaving quite arbitrarily or are making all the mistakes that are inevitable when the standards given us are all but totally unclear in expression. (I am inclined to think that this is about where we stand on the "insanity" test; see Chapter 6.)

All of this sounds uncomfortably close to philosophy, and is not the kind of thing congenial to me or, I dare say, to most of you. I have one excuse for taking you through such dull stuff, and for having the nerve to insist that you must try to follow it, going back and reading it over if necessary. My excuse I urge as clearly sufficient, for it is no less than the fact that, within a year or two, several hundred men and women may have electric current passed through their bodies until their eyeballs pop out and their brains are cooked, as a result of choices made under standards vulnerable to the objections I have just rehearsed. Let us understand these issues. Let us spare ourselves no pain of consideration before we see that occur—before we commit our society yet again to the policy of officially sanctioned killing.

For it is my assertion in this book that, in one way or another, the official choices—by prosecutors, judges, juries, and governors—that divide those who are to die from those who are to live are on the whole not made, and cannot be made, under standards that are consistently meaningful and clear, but that they are often made, and in the foreseeable future will continue often to be made, under no standards at all or under pseudo-standards without discoverable meaning. My further (and closely connected) assertion is that *mistake* in these choices is fated to occur.

At this early stage, I will anticipate only one objection—indeed, I am probably not anticipating, for it will doubtless already have arisen in your mind. Are not all human choices, including, particularly and most relevantly, all choices regarding criminal punishment, vulnerable to just these same objections?

The general answer must be "Of course they are; that is our predicament." (For a possible reservation, which I shall not try to argue, see the parenthetical paragraph ending Chapter 4.) I must therefore, to make my case, sustain the thesis that death is different—that the infliction of death by official choice ought to require a higher degree of clarity and precision in the governing standards than we can practicably require of all choices, even of choices for punishment. At this point I simply note that I take on myself that obligation and will try to redeem it in Chapter 4.

Chapter 3

Other Arguments about Capital Punishment

THE PURPOSE of this chapter is not to argue each issue in the capital punishment controversy, but rather to place the main thesis of the book, as it has just been stated, in relation to other issues in that controversy.

Let us take just the two main arguments commonly advanced in favor of the punishment of death—*retribution* and *deterrence*.

I know no way, finally, of effecting a meeting of minds, through reason, on the question whether sheer retribution is a worthy motive for action by the political society. I have never been able to get beyond the point of seeing here one of those ultimate clashes of value which cannot be resolved by argument. I am revolted by the idea of retribution through officially imposed death, just as I am revolted by the idea of poisoning for money; in neither case, in the end, am I able to *prove* to another person that

that person ought also to be revolted by either of these ideas or by both of them.

I do think, however, that those who believe in retribution as being in itself a valid ground for capital punishment may want to reexamine this belief if they are convinced that the thesis of this book is right. That thesis is that the penalty of death cannot be imposed, given the limitations of our minds and institutions, without considerable measures both of arbitrariness and of mistake. If this thesis is right, then in the full context the retribution question takes on what seems to me a new form. One must now ask oneself whether the moral value of sheer retribution is sufficient to justify not only the infliction of death in accordance with clear standards and without error, but also the infliction of death without clear standards and by mistake. No one can establish by proof that an affirmative answer to the altered question is wrong; perhaps it may be thought that, in the moral order, the exaction of vengeance is so indispensable a good that one must continue to exact vengeance even though one has faced the fact that this exaction is sometimes irrational and sometimes positively mistaken. I confess I cannot conceive the psychological possibility of such a conclusion, on the part of a normal person, but that is different from being able to prove it is wrong. As to the retribution value, then, what the thesis of this book does, if it is a true thesis, is to change the frame of reference in which the decision about the suitableness of the retribution motive must be made.

The other (and in modern days more accepted) argument for capital punishment is that it *deters* certain highly undesirable conduct. Here I think the thesis of this book has something to contribute on a logical or rational level.

It would be well first to recapitulate, without anything like full argument, the present state of the "deterrence" controversy.

First, it must be noted that what we are talking about is *not* whether the threat of punishment deters people from crime. The question, much more specific than that, is whether the threat of *death* is of significantly greater deterrent force than the threat of *long imprisonment*. How does this question now stand?

I think the answer has to be that, after all possible inquiry, including the probing of all possible methods of inquiry, we do not know, and for systematic and easily visible reasons cannot know, what the truth about this "deterrent" effect may be. We know that, on raw data, there has been somewhat more homicide in capital punishment states than in non-capital punishment states. But we cannot draw any valid conclusions from this, for factors other than the punishment system may easily explain the difference. The general problem that blocks knowledge here is that no adequately controlled experiment or observation is possible or (so far as we can see) ever will be possible. We have to use uncontrolled data from society itself, outside any laboratory. When we do that, there are two basic modes of procedure. One can compare, say, homicide statistics in states that, respectively, have or do not have capital punishment, over the same period of time. Or one can compare homicide rates in the same state, before and after the abolition or reinstitution of capital punishment.

The inescapable flaw is, of course, that social conditions in any state are not constant through time, and that social conditions are not the same in any two states. If an effect were observed (and the observed effects, one way or another, are not large) then one could not at all tell

whether any of this effect is attributable to the presence or
absence of capital punishment. A "scientific"—that is to
say, a soundly based—conclusion is simply impossible,
and no methodological path out of this tangle suggests
itself. When I last sampled this enormous literature, I
found two scholars were arguing over where the "burden
of proof" lay—whether, that is to say, the man who asserts
that capital punishment deters has to prove this
proposition or lose out, or whether the man who asserts
that it does *not* deter has to prove *this* proposition or lose
out. When you observe that an argument is in that
posture, you can be very sure that neither side has a
convincing case. Nobody is arguing about where the
"burden of proof" lies with respect to the assertion that
families of five with incomes under $4000 are on the whole
less well nourished than those with incomes over $20,000.

  Nor does "common sense" help. In the first place,
one of the soundest maxims of "common sense" is that
one is to look for and respect *evidence,* acknowledging as
unsolved those problems which the best evidence leaves
unsolved. "Common sense," moreover, has little to say
about the state of mind of people meditating murder or
rape; you or I might think the chance of death would
"deter" us more than would the chance of imprisonment—but neither I nor most of my readers have ever
seriously meditated murder or rape, and in fact we have
no basis for a "common sense" judgment in this matter.

  To go into deeper but still charted water, suicide is
one of the half-dozen chief killers in the United States,
ranking up somewhere near heart disease and automobile
accidents. If tens on tens of thousands of people want, or
think they want, to die, how unlikely is it that some of
them—disturbed as most of them are—might, consciously or unconsciously, pick the commission of a capital

crime as a means of suicide? (It often doesn't work, but that is true of all kinds of suicide attempts.) The possibility cannot be dismissed that capital punishment may in this way stimulate homicide. We just don't know.

On all scores, then, the "deterrence" question is wide open and will, as far as anyone can see, remain wide open indefinitely. The connection with the thesis of this book is clear. If this thesis—that we do not and cannot administer the penalty of death without arbitrariness and mistake—is true, some might think we ought nevertheless to go on administering it if there were a clear case for its saving innocent lives by deterring homicide. There is, however, no case for the proposition that any such effect is to be attributed to capital punishment. We are entirely free to abolish capital punishment on the ground that it is not and cannot be rationally administered, without any fear, or at least any fear warranted by proof or experience, that any innocent life would thereby be endangered.

When we turn from the two usual arguments in *favor* of capital punishment—retribution and deterrence—to the other side, we find, above all, that the *cruelty* of it is what its opponents hate—the cruelty of death, the cruelty of the manner of death, the cruelty of waiting for death, and the cruelty to the innocent persons attached by affection to the condemned—unless, of course, he has no relatives and no friends, a fairly common condition on death row. (I do not intend to broach at this point the question whether, as a matter of *law*, death is a "cruel and unusual punishment" within the meaning of the Eighth Amendment to the national Constitution; whatever the answer to that question may be, no sane person can doubt that the agony of waiting and of execution is cruel in the colloquial sense.) Here again, the connection with the thesis of this book is clear. One might decide (though I never could) that the infliction of this suffering is justified when it is inflicted on the *right* person—the person selected by the invariant and correct application of *clear* standards, set up by society through its constitutional forms. It would, I think, take a much hardier mind to conclude that this suffering may legitimately or desirably be inflicted on the basis of *unclear* standards, or no standards, with mistake, in the long run, a certainty. And it must be added that cruelty itself is greater when the arbitrariness or the mistake is visible to the condemned person, as must sometimes be the case. To sum up, if the nature of our institutions—and, indeed, of any institutions we can project—is such that the choice for death must often be standardless or mistaken, then the retribution question, the deterrence question, and the cruelty question all take on a different form and must be rethought. Is retribution a moral imperative when it is to fall on some persons arbitrarily chosen or chosen by mistake? Are we justified in using "deterrence" as an excuse for the execution of some persons chosen arbitrarily or by mistake when there is no affirmative case whatever for the reality of the "deterrence" effect? Are we justified in inflicting very great suffering when that suffering is to fall on some persons chosen arbitrarily or by mistake? If the thesis of this book is right, then those are the forms that must be taken by the three cardinal questions about capital punishment. I submit that every member of our society lies under the moral duty of deciding whether I am right in the contention that capital punishment cannot be administered without arbitrariness and mistake—and under the duty, if I am judged to be right in this, of rethinking each of the above three questions in the light of this thesis.

Chapter *4*

The Problem of Other Forms of Punishment

STARTING with the next chapter, I shall take up one by one the steps at which choice is made for death or life, and I shall try to show that each of these steps contains—and must contain—a component of arbitrariness and a potentiality for mistake unacceptable in a decision for the death of a person. I have already mentioned, though very briefly, that much the same things could be said of the very same steps when the decision made, say, is between five years and ten years in the penitentiary—when the decision, that is to say, has in any way to do with the quantity and kind of punishment or indeed with the question whether punishment shall be imposed at all. Since I have neither hope nor desire of persuading you that criminal punishment ought not to be administered at all, and since it is my thesis that there ineradicably inheres in our system an arbitrariness and a susceptibility to mistake which is absolutely unacceptable where the punishment is death, I must (as I said at the end of Chapter 2) take on the task of persuading you that death is different—that we ought not to accept, with respect to the death penalty, the arbitrariness and fallibility in decision which we must accept, and no doubt will go on accepting, with regard to other punishment. (This is not to say that I am entirely happy with the degree of standardless discretion and fallibility in decision which mark the administration of punishment less than death, but that is another matter, of much greater complexity, perhaps to be taken up at another time.)

Is death different? Are there grounds for requiring, as to the death penalty, greater certainty, both in standards and of correctness, than as to other penalties? I shall first discuss this question as a question of policy and then try to show that our legal system has in fact responded by accepting, in many ways, the specialness of death and the appropriateness of requiring, for death, more careful procedures than for any lesser punishment.

Plainly, any civilized system of punishments has to rank some punishments as more severe than others. It is very hard to conceive of any system in which this distinction is not felt and followed. Sometimes the distinction is very plain because it is a purely quantitative distinction, on a single scale; ten years in prison is a more severe punishment than sixty days in jail; a ten-dollar fine is a less severe punishment than a ten-thousand-dollar fine. Sometimes the distinction is qualitative, and hence a little harder to handle. Generally, in our culture, imprisonment is considered more severe than a fine. It might be questioned whether a ten-day jail sentence is a more or a less severe punishment than a ten-thousand-dollar fine, and the answer might well vary with the circumstances of the defendant, but the question is a real one.

Where does death stand on this scale, or on this set of scales? I should have thought that our culture had committed itself beyond doubt, and in the most unequivocal manner, to the proposition that death is a far more severe penalty than imprisonment. This is confirmed from every side. The penalty of death is reserved for the most serious and detested crimes. "Commutation" always means the commuting of a death sentence to a prison sentence; we would think someone had taken leave of his senses who spoke of the "commutation" of a prison sentence to a death sentence or who could, for example, use the term "recommendation of mercy" to mean recommendation of death instead of prison. A Stoic philosopher might want to argue this point, but we are dealing with a real system in the real world; grades of severity have to be judged, in such a frame, as they are judged by the culture in which they exist, and few things are clearer than the fact that our culture sees death as more severe than imprisonment, by an order-of-magnitude jump. This is confirmed by everything from the most famous soliloquy in Hamlet to the desperate battle of condemned people to be allowed to live in prison rather than to be put to death.

To the uniqueness of extinction, to the uniqueness of the agony of anticipating extinction, to death's unique destruction of all hope, must be added, when we are talking about death as a socially chosen punishment, the uniquely irrevocable character of killing. It is of course true that in some sense (as Bernard Shaw, I believe, pointed out) imprisonment is irrevocable. Everything that is done or suffered is irrevocable; even a day's happiness is irrevocable. But it is a blurred vision indeed that cannot see a radically different *kind* of irrevocability in death. Time spent in prison through mistake cannot be given back *in specie*, but some compensation can be attempted, as the law attempts it for many wrongs, all of them "irrevocable" in the same sense as that in which imprisonment is irrevocable. A prison sentence may be shortened if the behavior of the prisoner seems to warrant this, or if cooled judgment makes the originally awarded sentence seem too harsh. Prison itself may furnish some opportunities for choice and some chance (as Camus has so perceptively remarked) for the criminal's making amends. If a wrong determination on "sanity" seems to have been made, a prisoner may be transferred to medical facilities. Some or all prisoners may have some hope of betterment in the conditions under which they must live. Imprisonment, then, though very bitter, and though irrevocable in the same sense as are all other sufferings and even happenings, offers many chances for change, many windows of hope.

Having seen this, we can see at once that death *is* different, that it is irrevocable in quite a distinct sense from the general irrevocability of all happenings. If a mistake of any kind is discovered, it is too late. In every way and for every purpose, it is too late.

Now to the second step: Ought higher standards of clarity and certainty in administration to be required for the imposing of severer penalties?

Here again, the consensus of civilization seems clear. Parking tickets have to be disposed of summarily; practically speaking, you just pay the man the two dollars and fight the charge only if you want to make some kind of point. The imposition of a ten-day jail sentence obviously does not call for the kind of "due process' that ought to be furnished when what is in question is a ten-year prison sentence. If death, as the culture unambiguously assumes, is by far the worst punishment, then the requirements of "due process" for death may reasonably be set higher than the requirements of "due process" for other punishments.

All this would seem fairly obvious, and I rehearse it all because even the obvious ought not to be left unsaid when it is a step in an argument about killing, and because it is essential that I meet squarely the objection that all I have to say about arbitrariness and mistake in a death case is true as to all decision.

As irrefutable confirmation of all the above, we ought now to note that the strictly legal side of our culture has taken abundant note of the differentness of death as a punishment and of the consequent differentness of "due process" requirements when death is the stake in play; the relevance of legal provisions here is that they authoritatively establish our collective judgment on this question.

Our legal system is simply saturated, at all levels, with the ideas that requirements of fairness, certainty, and so on—all the things we mean when we say "due process of law"—vary with the seriousness of the interest at stake, and that, as a corollary, imposition of the penalty of death carries with it a more exacting requirement than other punitive action of the political society. As to the first of these ideas, the Supreme Court, as recently as 1972, has remarked: "It has been said so often by this Court and others as not to require citation of authority that due process is flexible and calls for such procedural protection as the particular situation demands."

But of course practice throughout the country and the world has always illustrated this obvious truth. No traffic court affords the kind of "due process" that is given the felony defendant. No procedure for fixing a real property tax assessment has the safeguards that surround a proceeding that may result in the loss of one's home.

We are here interested mostly in the recognition, by our own legal system, of the heightened "due process" requirements that move into place *when life is at stake.* All the state legal systems in one way or another—by requiring jury unanimity, by forbidding pleas of guilty to a capital offense, by providing for automatic appeals, and so on—have recognized this distinction, quite without compulsion from the national Supreme Court. But when such compulsion was needed it has been forthcoming. For many years our federal Supreme Court required of the states that they invariably assign counsel in capital cases, while leaving the question of counsel in noncapital cases open to variation based on special circumstances; the fact that at last the Court decided counsel should be required in all serious criminal cases does not impair the force of the earlier cases as establishing national recognition of the immense difference between imprisonment and death. On the other side of the coin, the Supreme Court has several times upheld, as not violating any federal guarantee, state laws imposing more stringent requirements for trial in capital cases than in other cases.

The late Mr. Justice Frankfurter, in a concurring opinion, once said:

These cases involve the validity of procedural conditions for determining the commission of a crime in fact punishable by death. The taking of life is irrevocable. It is in capital cases especially that the balance of conflicting interests must be weighted most heavily in favor of the procedural safeguards of the Bill of Rights.

The late Mr. Justice Harlan, concurring in the same case, said:

So far as capital cases are concerned, I think they stand on quite a different footing than other offenses. In such cases the law is especially sensitive to demands for that procedural fairness which inheres in a civilian trial where the judge and trier of fact are not responsive to the command of the convening authority. I do not concede that whatever process is "due" an offender faced with a fine or a prison sentence necessarily satisfies the requirements of the Constitution in a capital case.

I have quoted from these two Justices because they, perhaps more than any others in the last few decades, represent a principled conservatism in respect of the function of the Supreme Court in reviewing state criminal cases—and they were both exceedingly learned and astute lawyers. A distinction to which they so unequivocally committed themselves can hardly need further validation.

Now let me wrap this chapter up by reminding you how all this ties in with the main thesis of the book. That thesis is that our criminal-justice concepts and institutions cannot administer the punishment of death without a measure of arbitrariness, and a measure of susceptibility to mistake, unacceptable when life or death is the issue. A possible major objection to this thesis would be that this arbitrariness, and this susceptibility to mistake, are just as great when imprisonment, and not death, is the stake, and that we cannot consistently, therefore, use this arbitrariness and mistake-proneness of the system to cause us to hold our hand on killing, since the very same considerations ought to cause us to hold our hand on *any* punishment—a result nobody now, if ever, realistically could advocate. The answer this chapter gives is, first, that the most obvious common sense would counsel that certainty and fixity of standards is more stringently requisite as penalties grow more serious; secondly, that our culture has for centuries unambiguously, and with good reason, looked on death as a more serious penalty than imprisonment; thirdly, that our legal system has—as a matter of practice and as a matter of constitutional law—committed itself to this distinction. We ought, I should suppose, to try to improve as much as we can the administration of *any* punishment. But we need not fear that we will have committed ourselves to the Utopian dream of a world without any criminal justice if we conclude that our system of administering criminal justice simply will not decently do as a system for separating out those who are to die.

Let us go on, then, to consider the stages of decision, from freedom on the street to the electric chair, and ask ourselves whether each of these stages is or can be made free enough from arbitrariness and error to make us willing to ordain that some shall be killed at the end of this terrible series of choice.

(I have chosen not to argue in this chapter the possibility that the life-or-death decision, because of the emotion that swirls around it, and because of the perhaps unique difficulty of putting into clear words the concepts that are to govern the life-or-death choice, may really be *more* mistake-prone and *less* amenable to rational standardization than decisions made in other parts of the criminal law. I avoid this argument, though I think there may be much in it, because it cannot be made without some appeal to intuition. What has been said quite suffices for sustaining the burden this chapter takes on.)

Chapter 5

The Decisions on Charging and on Plea-Bargaining

WHEN WE LOOK at criminal justice as a *process* rather than as a set of rules associating certain punishments with certain crimes, the concept of rigorously mandatory linkage between act and punishment fades out. It begins to fade when we consider the process of *charging*. How and by whom is it decided what crime to charge, after the raw factual picture—or, more accurately, the raw evidence, in hand and anticipated—is digested in part and in part forecasted?

The rough answer (not subject to sufficient qualification to make analysis of the qualifications here worthwhile) is that the *prosecutor* makes this decision, and that his decision is within large limits "discretion-

ary"—subject to no clearly statable rule, but formed, even
by the most conscientious of prosecutors, on the basis of
an open-ended series of factors, such as an estimate of
difficulties of proof or a belief that a charge of the
maximum offense that might be proved would result in an
unduly severe punishment given the circumstances, and
so on. It is the ". . . and so on" that is most important, for
there is no rule to bar entry of any noncorrupt
consideration—and the occasional entry of a corrupt
consideration is exceedingly hard to establish. The
United States Court of Appeals for the Fifth Circuit, in a
widely approved case, has said, "The discretionary power
. . . in determining whether a prosecution shall be
commenced or maintained may well depend upon
matters of policy wholly apart from any question of
probable cause." [United States v. Cox, 342 F.2d 167, 171
(5th Cir.) *certiorari denied,* 381 U.S. 926] *A fortiori,* the
decision as to what charge to bring is likewise discretionary.

I am not going to come down very hard on this stage
of the process, because its part in administering the death
penalty in the future, if that penalty is reinstated, is hard
to predict. Probably up to now it has not played much part
in capital cases; these are all very serious, and the
tendency has been to charge the maximum offense, since
leniency might be anticipated further down the line. On
the other hand, we are told by a leading authority on the
"charging" decision (Miller) that (as we easily might
guess) one of the standard uses of "discretion" in charging
is the avoidance of "punishment harm that administrative
officials regard as too severe . . . because conviction of
the maximum offense carries a statutory mandatory
minimum sentence. . . ." Now some of the new
death-penalty statutes do seek to make capital punish-

ment mandatory for certain described offenses; it would seem anticipatable then, that the discretionary power to charge a lesser offense would sometimes be used to avoid this severe result. If a bill in a certain state, for example, becomes law, death by hanging will be *mandatory* for one who "*recklessly* causes the death of a law enforcement officer, Corrections employee or fireman while such officer is in the lawful performance of his duties. . . ." Is it necessary to construct an elaborate hypothetical case to convince anybody that the killing of a policeman, in line of duty, not by intention but merely "recklessly," might sometimes occur in such a way that it would be simply absurd, as well as incredibly cruel, to *hang* the "reckless" person? I would think it inevitable that, with such statutes in force, many cases must occur wherein conduct, though plainly falling within the statutory language, and plainly deserving punishment, equally plainly could hardly be seen by a sane person as deserving death. It would seem nearly inevitable, then, that prosecutors would use some common sense in charging, just as they now do with respect to offenses carrying minimum terms of imprisonment. But that "common sense," however much we might applaud its exercise in the individual case, is subject to no rule of law, but is exercised "arbitrarily," on the basis of "discretion" alone. Nor can this practicably be changed, for change would require the condition, contrary to fact and to possibility, that we know in advance of trial, or even of charge, of what offense the accused person is actually guilty.

Let me go just a little further into this (even though the "charging" choice may not be of cardinal importance) because it is in a way paradigmatic of a problem that entirely pervades any attempt to take "discretion"—which always to some extent covers arbitrariness—out of criminal law. The only tool available for doing this is the *verbal* description of some course of conduct, and the rigorous association, with conduct fitting that form of words, of a fixed (or minimum) penalty. And the invariant truth is that no verbal description ever succeeds in anticipating all the special (and often highly important) variations in circumstances that may occur. I remember discussing with some lawmakers a proposed statute which would impose a *mandatory* sentence of twenty years on something called "hijacking" an airplane. I cannot quote this proposed law exactly, but it defined this crime, approximately, as "using force, or the threat of force, to cause any person lawfully in possession and control of an aircraft to divert that aircraft to any destination other than the one intended and desired by such person in lawful control and possession," and for doing that you *had* to get twenty years. That sounds just right if you happen to be thinking (as most people then were thinking) of the well-publicized cases of hijacking of passenger jets for political purposes. But I interposed the question, "What about a guest in his friend's Piper Cub, owned and piloted by the friend, who says 'I've got a girl I want to see in Akron, and if you don't put this thing down there, I'll beat you up when we land'?" Punishment? Of course; you can't fool around with airplanes. But *twenty years*? I never found anybody who thought that would be right.

We are dealing with something eternal, or at least humanly eternal. It passes the wit of man to anticipate all circumstances in drawing a law—even all those circumstances which would make application of the law, as drawn, ridiculous. If strictly mandatory death-penalty statutes are enacted, the law will give somewhere; one of the places where it *can* give is at the stage of *charging*, and I would expect to see many cases of prosecutors' charging less than they might have proved, to avoid the danger of this most drastic of sentences. But those decisions are not subject to any rule, and cannot—for the reason given above—practicably be made subject to any rule.

The part that will be played in future by prosecutors' unbridled "discretion" in charging is, as I hope I have candidly indicated, conjectural (though not, I think, beyond probable conjecture). The next (and closely associated) stage—that of "plea-bargaining"—is not conjectural. By far the majority of our criminal cases are handled by plea-bargaining. TV shows, where the case goes to a hard-fought trial, don't perhaps instruct us adequately on this, but everybody knows about it down at the courthouse. What is plea-bargaining?

At the conclusion of the "charging" process, just discussed, a defendant stands accused of one or more crimes, and if no intermediate process intervenes he will go on trial for those crimes. For simplicity, let us use just one—say, "assault with a deadly weapon." On TV, the next step is the trial. At the real courthouse, in a very large percentage of the cases, the next step is a bargaining session or sessions between the prosecutor (or an assistant) and the defendant's lawyer. As in the "charging" process, the prosecutor's bargaining stance is conditioned by an open-ended series of factors—the likelihood of winning on the serious charge already filed, the tax on the trial resources of the county, the defendant's prior "respectability" (a term I am not making up but am taking from a principal authority on the subject), political pressure, and so forth. The decision to offer a "plea" to the defendant—to let him plead guilty to a lesser offense than the one charged (maybe "simple assault" in the example given) and so reduce the possible punishment—is thus made without obedience to statable rule. It is made, in fact, on the basis of just that kind of ruleless "discretion" that the Furman case seemed to be condemning when the life-or-death choice was made by a jury.

Yet this is one of the critical (and almost always exceedingly important) official choices between life and death, made on the defendant's way from the street to the electric chair. And it is utterly visionary to think it can be eliminated or reduced to rule. Our entire criminal-law system lives and moves and has its being in the "plea-bargaining" institution. An impossible tax would be placed on our resources if we had to hold full trials for all the people who now are induced to plead guilty, by a promise of what is in effect a limitation on possible punishment.

Nor is there any practicable way to reduce this process to rule. Just as with the "charging" process, reduction to rule of the "plea-bargaining" process would require the impossible—an *adjudication* of the exact degree of guilt of the defendant, in advance of trial, or, as a rather inefficient and quite problematic alternative, forcing the prosecutor to go to trial in every case on the maximum charge barely suggested by the known evidence, without regard to his own estimate of the probabilities of conviction. And either of these "rules," besides being absurd and productive of needless harm, would tax our resources beyond any point our society will possibly stand for.

So, within any foreseeable future, one of the absolutely crucial decisions for life or death—the decision whether to offer the defendant a chance to plead guilty to a noncapital offense—will be made administratively, on the basis of administrative discretion, without clear standards in law.

This is emphatically not to say that these decisions

either have been or will be in the main corrupt or tricky. (Nor can it be said, people being what they are, that some of them will not be corrupt—motivated, for example, by political considerations or by the state of public feeling as to certain crimes.) Rulelessness is something different from corruptness. But rulelessness will not do for what is probably the most widely significant choice separating the doomed from those who must go to prison.

There is in this process, too, the possibility of mistake. For example, one of the factors that commonly affect the prosecutor's bargaining stance in the "plea-bargaining" process is the defendant's prior record in the broadest sense—not only his prior convictions but also suspicions, associations, and the like. Since no procedure of any kind is prescribed for the ascertainment or assessment of this material, mistake is easily possible.

But this kind of mistake is not the most serious fault with plea-bargaining in the death-penalty case. The most serious is that, inevitably, some are spared while others are pushed on along the road to execution, without any *rule* to govern the choice—only such prudential and rough-equity considerations as may move the particular prosecutor.

One ought not to finish on plea-bargaining without mentioning the role of the *defendant's* lawyer. The person in custody accused of capital crime is very likely to be frightened and not in any shape to know what is best for him. More often than not, he does not at all understand the criminal justice system. (These facts, as if they needed it, have received confirmation in many judgments of the Supreme Court.) He is thus heavily dependent on the advice of his lawyer—often an assigned counsel or an overworked public defender. This lawyer too, having no clear guides in the form of rules, and required to assess a situation in a hurry, may make a mistake, and if his mistake consists in advising his client not to accept the chance to plead guilty to a noncapital offense, this may be the really relevant choice for death made at this stage. I would estimate, however, that the prosecutor's choice whether or not to offer such a chance is far more often the significant one.

(One truly parenthetical but very important point ought to be added about the connection of plea-bargaining with capital punishment. In a case that by any stretch of evidence and imagination might be capital, the threat of the death penalty, even as a bare possibility, puts in the prosecutor's hand, as he bargains, a counter of something like infinite weight, often virtually forcing the defendant to plead guilty to something, even though the chances may be great that he would have been acquitted—and virtually forcing his lawyer to advise him to plead, lest he himself, the lawyer, be responsible for his client's execution. Indeed, in view of the very small number of persons actually executed in recent times (some two dozen people a year, before the "stays" described in Chapter 1 took hold) it is a not unreasonable conjecture that these people died, in great part, *pour encourager les autres* to plead guilty to a lesser offense than capital, without invariable regard to provable guilt. I do not think this a desirable thing, but I drop it here, for it is not connected with my principal thesis.)

Chapter 6

The Trial and Verdict

If the defendant has been charged with a capital offense, and if no plea-bargain has been arranged, then he goes on trial for his life, usually before a jury. That jury will have at least one, and usually two, things to determine. First, it must determine whether (*and of what*) the defendant is guilty. Secondly, if it finds the defendant guilty of a crime which *may* be punishable by death, it must, under many of the new death-penalty statutes now being enacted in the states, determine whether the penalty is to be death or life imprisonment. This chapter will deal with the first of these functions—the "guilty or not-guilty" function. The next chapter will take up the sentence-choice function.

The "guilty or not-guilty" function of the jury has two aspects, though they are in practice inseparable. In a capital case, the jury must determine whether the defendant is guilty of the capital offense—punishable by death—with which he is charged. But in very many cases its finding of "not guilty" of the capital offense may be accompanied by a finding of "guilty" of some "lesser offense." Let us again get this concept clear. If one person kills another person and is charged with willful murder, a jury may well find that he indeed killed the other man but did so recklessly without "willfulness." In such a case, under proper instructions from the judge, the jury may find the man "not guilty" of murder but nevertheless "guilty" of "negligent homicide" or "manslaughter." (Both the terminology and the exact rules will vary from state to state, but some such set of possibilities exists in every state.)

Pragmatically, what this means is that a jury can very considerably manipulate penalties; it is very often not faced by the choice of either freeing the defendant or convicting him on the capital charge. Ideally, the jury makes this choice solely on the basis of the "facts"; in the case put, it simply registers, by its verdict, its conclusion on the factual question, "Was this killing 'deliberate' or was it simply 'reckless'?" But there are two enormous flaws in this neat picture. First, the "factual" question (like the one in the example) may be exceedingly difficult to determine by evidence; this means, obviously, that mistake is easily possible. Secondly, there is in actual practice no way to keep a jury from finding a defendant "not guilty" on the capital charge but "guilty" of the lesser included offense, whatever its secret views may be on the actual facts; indeed, the law usually gives juries great latitude on this. If we add into all this the natural human tendency to see facts and to evaluate evidence in a manner leading to a desired conclusion, it becomes, to say the very least, easily possible that the jury, which on this matter is practically uncontrollable, may find any defendant "not guilty" on the capital but "guilty" on the lesser charge, on the basis of whatever it may regard— whether humanely or corruptly—as circumstances in mitigation, or even on the basis of appealing personal characteristics in the defendant. This result, like the decision of the prosecutor to accept a plea of guilty in the plea-bargaining process, sounds good; somebody escapes death. The trouble is that if you turn the coin around, somebody else *suffers* death because the jury did *not* find him guilty of a lesser offense rather than of the capital charge. And if the jury's *milder* verdict may be a function of its sympathies, then its *sterner* verdict, by inevitable logic, may be a function of its *lack* of sympathy. And it must be remembered that this alternative, open to the jury, is not effectively controllable, but may mask any amount of purely "discretionary" decision. In the nature of the case it is not possible to say how often this happens; we have no independent procedure for determining whether the jury was *factually* right. But I do not know anybody familiar with the process who thinks the possibility I have here sketched not a genuine one, often realized in fact.

But, for simplicity, let us turn back to that aspect of the jury's work which consists in the simple determination of "guilty" or "not guilty" on the capital charge. The performance of this task carries with it two principal problems. First, the determination of questions of sheer fact is not easy; mistake is bound to occur now and then in the long run. Secondly, the *definitions* of capitally punishable murder often employ verbiage and concepts exceedingly difficult to explain and apply.

As to the first of these difficulties, it is enough to say that juries, at best and even ideally, are not infallible; to be fallible means to *make a mistake* sometimes. A very important addition is the reminder that the questions of sheer *fact* which a jury must determine in a capital case extend over a range both enormously wider and far more difficult than the question "Did the defendant kill the deceased?" I must emphasize this again and again. In the movies and in the press, "mistake" seems usually to mean "The jury found that he did it, but now it turns out that it was done not by him but by somebody else." Even on the level of sheer mistake as to physical fact, the array of possible errors is enormously more extended than this. The first piece of paper that happened to catch my eye on my desk as I was writing the above sentence contained a digest of an Arizona case in which the critical question was not whether the defendant shot the deceased, which was conceded, but whether the deceased threatened the defendant with a knife, so that the shooting was in self-defense. Since, it seems, only the two of them were present, the evidence consisted only of the defendant's own testimony, plus the reputation of the deceased for carrying a knife, and the finding of a knife—which finding, incidentally, had in the actual case *been concealed* by the prosecutor! Quite obviously, a jury can easily make a mistake in a case of that sort. It can even more easily make a mistake as to the endless questions of "state of mind" and "intention" which it must find on.

But the possibility of mistake in the "guilty" or "not guilty" choice does not end with mistake either as to physical or unproblematically describable psychological fact. The jury is also called upon to pronounce upon mixed questions of fact and law, questions that have puzzled the most astute legal minds. One of these, perennially with us, is "premeditation." "Premeditation" is very often a defining characteristic of capital murder. If "meditation" connotes some duration of thought, then "premeditation" might be expected to denote thought about the killing over a considerable time. But judges have repeatedly said that the premediation need not be of any particular length; a moment is enough. On the other hand, "premeditation" is not the same as "intent to kill."

If you try to run down, in standard treatises or in the cases, the distinctions in state of mind required for the different "degrees" of murder or for distinguishing between the traditional offenses of "murder" and "manslaughter," the first thing you find is that the solution of the exceedingly difficult psychological problems involved varies from state to state. You also find that the "definitions" proffered are intelligible enough when extreme examples are used; it is easy to see that a long-planned poisoning for the sake of insurance money is "premeditated," while a killing in the very first flare of passion on discovering one's spouse in bed with somebody else is probably not "premeditated"—though, on the basis of some doctrine, it could be. The difficulty of course occurs in the close cases which actually come to court in great number. We are told, for example, that "premeditation" requires no particular duration of time, yet that frequently the line of demarcation between first and second degree murder is drawn by putting into the second-degree class (not punishable by death) *intentional* killings without "premeditation." We are invited to distinguish between "murder" and "manslaughter" by reference to "greater" or "less" *measures* of passion. (How do you measure passion?) The statutes and the literature abound in such archaic terms as "affray" or "lying in wait." In sum, in a great many close cases, no matter how patiently the judge tries to explain to the jury that which he himself only cloudily understands, the net result must be that twelve laypersons have no alternative to using their general sense of the equities of the matter. But this means that these purported rules, at the crucial line of separation between those who are to die and those who are to live, conceal a discretion which, however benevolent, is to all intents and purposes standardless.

But the most crucial point is reached when we get to the "insanity" problem. In every state, in some manner, "insanity" is a defense to a charge of capital (or indeed other) crime. If the defendant can satisfy the jury that his act bore some legally defined relation to "insanity" as the law defines it, he escapes conviction—usually facing compulsory hospitalization instead—hospitalization that is often not much, if any, more desirable than prison.

There have been three major approaches by law to the "insanity" problem: the so-called "M'Naghten" rule, the "irresistible impulse" rule, and the recent "Durham" rule. (The first and third are named after the cases in which they were enunciated. The Durham rule has not won any acceptance.)

The M'Naghten rule says that one is relieved of criminal responsibility if, as a result of "disease of the mind" he does not "know the nature and quality of the act" or, "if he did know it . . . he did not know he was doing what was wrong." Every word in this rule, except the prepositions and definite articles, has been problematical. Dean Abraham Goldstein, one of the greatest living authorities on the subject, says, for example, that the "word 'know' has been at the center of the controversy. . . ." Does it mean "formal cognition" or "emotional awareness"? How about "wrong"? Does it mean "morally wrong" or "legally wrong"? Dean Goldstein says that the "word is generally given to the jury without explanation." And so on. (Dean Goldstein, incidentally, makes a brilliant and in my view irrefutable case for the proposition that the M'Naghten rule need not have had the constricting effect on the "insanity defense" that has been given it. But I do not understand him to say that it can be made into a precise instrument for separating those who should be held responsible from those who should not—still less for separating those who are to live from those who are to die.)

The second "rule" is the rule of the "irresistible impulse." Here again we run into a deep philosophic problem. To the determinist, all "impulses"—indeed all urges eventuating in action, whether "sudden" or not—are "irresistible"; this is shown by the fact that they were not resisted, for to the determinist that which happens is that which must happen, through the working of antecedent causes. Since this won't do, where do we draw the line? No change in verbal form can get around the central problem, and no satisfactory way has ever been devised of communicating to the jury the meaning of a standard carrying about with it this basic philosophic difficulty.

Thirdly, the originally much-acclaimed "Durham" rule, announced for the District of Columbia in 1954, not generally adopted elsewhere, and now abandoned even in the District, uses the word "product" as the key verbal symbol: Was the act the "product" of "mental disease" or "mental defect"? But the cause-and-effect relationship contained in the word "product" is utterly ambiguous, and "mental disease" is, as Dean Goldstein points out, an exceedingly problematic concept.

Probably in part as a result of the ferment caused by the putting forward of the Durham rule, later attempts have been made, notably by the American Law Institute, to put words together that will communicate to a jury, for guidance of its action, a satisfactory "insanity" test. All this effort may very well have resulted (or may promise to result) in there reaching the jury more and better testimony on "insanity," and on the jury's working within a freer range in using this testimony. But few now pretend—and the pretense fades as knowledge grows— that any "rule" is or can be without a very substantial component of "discretion." This, like "mercy," sounds good, unless you are on the wrong end of it. "Discretion," in that case, means that you are being executed without at all knowing why—and to the rest of us it means that we are executing people without being able to say clearly why we picked just these people to execute. On the whole, I find no reason to modify what I said several years ago in the Morris Ames Soper Lecture at the University of Maryland:

We are committed, as a society, not to execute people whose action is attributable to what we call "insanity" or who are mentally incapable of standing trial, or who are what we call "insane" at the time of execution. As to the second and third of these, little need be said. In judging a defendant's capacity to participate effectively at his trial, we take into account neither low intelligence, unless, perhaps, he is clinically an imbecile, nor cultural inaccessibility, to him, of any understanding of the proceedings, just as we disregard his lack of financial resources to engage able counsel or to set afoot investigation that might clear him. As to insanity at the time of execution, this is so familiar a phenomenon in fact, and the procedure for ascertaining and acting upon it is generally so defective, that the thing speaks for itself. Obviously, mistake is easily possible in either of these two respects, and doubtless often occurs. Let me focus on so-called "insanity" as a defense.

Once again, let us remember that we have committed ourselves not to kill by law, or even to punish, anyone who satisfies certain criteria as to the connection of "insanity" with the commission of the act. Yet the astounding fact is that, having made this commitment, for what must be the most imperative moral reasons, we cannot state these criteria in any understandable form, in any form satisfying to the relevant specialists or comprehensible to either judge or jury, despite repeated and earnest trials. The upshot of the best writing on the subject is that we have so far failed in defining exculpatory "insanity," and that success is nowhere in sight. Yet we have to assume, unless the whole thing has been a solemn frolic, that we execute some people, and put others into medical custody, because we think that the ones we execute fall on one side of this line, and the others on the other side.

I am talking about mistake, and it is hard to apply the concept of *mistake*, of rightness or wrongness, to the application of criteria of the quality we have succeeded in expressing, criteria which we do not ourselves even pretend to understand. But what a fearful alternative faces us here! Either mistake is possible as to the application of such criteria, and therefore extremely likely to occur, given the quality of the criteria, or else the criteria themselves are quite meaningless, and mark no line. If the latter is true, then we are executing some people, and treating others medically, on an irrational basis.

It would not be surprising if this were so, for we are dealing here, in truth, with philosophic issues which philosophy has quite failed to resolve—issues of determinism, free will, and responsibility. But we are not debating these issues philosophically. We are putting some humans through inutterable agony on the basis of a pretense, nothing short of frivolous, that we have satisfactorily resolved these issues. How can we dare go on doing this?

I want now to digress, briefly, to cover a special problem which seems to fit here better than anywhere else. As I have worked on this lecture, I have, of course, talked it over with many people. I want to mention now one particular view which I have encountered several times. I have heard it said, by people I must respect, that they generally deplore the use of capital punishment, as to almost all killings—the *crime passionel*, the street-fight knifing, or even the fatal mugging for money—but that they believe a few crimes—the Sharon Tate murders, for example, or the multiple mad killings by Starkweather—to be so horrible as suitably to be atoned only by death. I introduce this special view at this very point in order to focus attention on the fact that it is precisely as to such crimes that we run the greatest chance of misapplication of the insanity "test" to which we must be taken solemnly to have committed ourselves. This is true, above all, for an intrinsic and inescapable reason. Where the killing is of a kind colloquially describable as mad, and actually is so described in newspaper headlines, where the crime exhibits a total wild departure from normality, we come exactly to the point where consideration of the insanity problem is at once most necessary and most difficult. The man who kills his wife's lover in a fit of rage is not necessarily mad at all. To call sane the man who, for no visible reason, walks into a barber shop with a Tommy gun and shoots a dozen barbers and customers, is to call into question our deepest assumptions as to what sanity, in social life, can possibly mean. We must, in such a case, face the issue of exculpatory insanity. But I have already reminded you that the tools we have elaborated for resolving it are about as useful as flamingoes are for playing croquet. In every case, therefore, of the supremely revolting murder, we face in particularly acute form the exculpatory insanity question, without adequate means, to say the very least, for answering it. How likely is it that we will answer it rightly? Before we frame our reply to that question, we have to face the further realistic fact that the issue of "insanity" is referred, with inadequate if not totally meaningless directions, to people who must, if they are normal, view the defendant with extremest abhorrence. I suggest that those people who disapprove of the death penalty in general, but who would apply it in such cases, ponder these facts.

(I should point out here, parenthetically, that it is only with respect to the punishment of death that our insane "insanity" rules do major damage. If a "sane" man is mistakenly classified as "insane," and confined indefinitely in a state hospital, then that is in itself a very heavy punishment. If an "insane" man is mistakenly classified as "sane," and sentenced to that indefinite imprisonment we call "life," then his condition can be, and is, reviewed medically from time to time, and he may be, and sometimes is, transferred to a hospital. The difference is of an altogether different order of magnitude from the difference between killing and not killing. I hope, also parenthetically, that I will not be taken to have implied that people like Starkweather could ever safely be turned loose, under any foreseeable state of the art of psychiatry.)

I would only draw the reader's attention to the last paragraph of this quotation. The "insanity" problem is a problem in prudent management from time to time, *until* we hit the death-penalty case. At that point the "insanity" problem changes character altogether and goes to the heart of our moral order.

Now I think I have said enough to show that the first verdict, the verdict that says "guilty" or "not guilty," and if "guilty" then "guilty of what," is arrived at by a process which invites and requires, at some points, the use of standardless discretion, however camouflaged, and which also is, at many points, susceptible of mistake—either mistake of fact or mistake in the application of standards (or pseudo-standards) to fact. This is not surprising. It would be very surprising if it were not so; modern insights into law have made it very plain that most if not all law has these characteristics. What is surprising is that we go on executing people as a consequence of the outcome of such a process, once we have seen into it.

Let us pass on to the second stage under many of the new capital-punishment statutes—the stage of explicit choice between death and imprisonment.

Chapter 7

The Sentence-Choice

THE MINIMUM MEANING of the 1972 Furman case (often referred to above) which declared unconstitutional the administration of capital punishment as up to then carried out, probably can be read (if one attends principally to the reasoning in the opinions of Stewart and White, the marginal Justices) as a condemnation of standardless discretion in *sentencing*—a discretion often lodged in the jury or judge. In the end, I hope to have convinced the reader that standardless discretion, as well as mistake-proneness, are not to be found only at the sentencing stage but permeate the whole series of choices that have to be made on the way from street to gallows; at least one more, "clemency," remains for the chapter after this. But it was natural for the states desiring somehow to retain capital punishment to try so to react as to answer specifically this objection of standardlessness in the jury's choice of sentence.

Reaction has taken two forms. In some states, the death penalty has been made mandatory for certain crimes; this entirely removes the "jury discretion" objection but of course does not alter any of the other difficulties heretofore discussed or the "clemency" difficulty discussed in the next chapter. With these newly "mandatory" states may be grouped those states continuing to seek to enforce capital punishment under "mandatory" statutes antedating the 1972 Furman case. (We may throw in here the odd case of North Carolina, where, over vigorous dissent, a bare majority of the state Supreme Court held that the Furman case had no other effect than to abolish the jury's power to recommend mercy, so that the penalty of death became mandatory in cases where it had previously been subject to jury reduction; this odd reasoning explains the grisly fact that there were at last count *forty persons* (twenty-five of them black) on death row in North Carolina alone, out of 114 in the nation—more than a third, in a state not at all known for its savagery.)

In some other states, a new stage in the process has been added, in an attempt to meet the Furman case's objection. (A few states already had this second stage.) After conviction of a capital felony, a second hearing is held, at the conclusion of which the jury (or the judge) decides between life and death. This decision is to be made, under these statutes, on the basis of certain "standards," and we can appraise the efficacy with which they meet the Furman case's objection, as I have interpreted that objection in the first paragraph of this chapter.

Let's look at the statute from Texas, here reproduced in its entirety, from the Texas Code of Criminal Procedure; I earnestly ask you to work through it with me, checking my back- and cross-references; they are not difficult—merely tedious—and perhaps the tedium will be relieved if you keep in mind what is at stake:

Art. 37.071.   Procedure in capital case

(a) Upon a finding that the defendant is guilty of a capital offense, the court shall conduct a separate sentencing proceeding to determine whether the defendant shall be sentenced to death or life imprisonment. The proceeding shall be conducted in the trial court before the trial jury as soon as practicable. In the proceeding, evidence may be presented as to any matter that the court deems relevant to sentence. This subsection shall not be construed to authorize the introduction of any evidence secured in violation of the Constitution of the United States or of the State of Texas. The state and the defendant or his counsel shall be permitted to present argument for or against sentence of death.

(b) On conclusion of the presentation of the evidence, the court shall submit the following issues to the jury:

(1) whether the conduct of the defendant that caused the death of the deceased was committed deliberately and with the reasonable expectation that the death of the deceased or another would result;

(2) whether there is a probability that the defendant would commit criminal acts of violence that would constitute a continuing threat to society; and

(3) if raised by the evidence, whether the conduct of the defendant in killing the deceased was unreasonable in response to the provocation, if any, by the deceased.

(c) The state must prove each issue submitted beyond a reasonable doubt, and the jury shall return a special verdict of "yes" or "no" on each issue submitted.

(d) The court shall charge the jury that:

(1) it may not answer any issue "yes" unless it agrees unanimously; and

(2) it may not answer any issue "no" unless 10 or more jurors agree.

(e) If the jury returns an affirmative finding on each issue submitted under this article, the court shall sentence the defendant to death. If the jury returns a negative finding on any issue submitted under this article, the court shall sentence the defendant to confinement in the Texas Department of Corrections for life.

(f) The judgment of conviction and sentence of death shall be subject to automatic review by the Court of Criminal Appeals within 60 days after certification by the sentencing court of the entire record unless time is extended an additional period not to exceed 30 days by the Court of Criminal Appeals for good cause shown. Such review by the Court of Crminal Appeals shall have priority over all other cases, and shall be heard in accordance with rules promulgated by the Court of Criminal Appeals.

Added by Acts 1973, 63rd Leg., p. 1125, ch. 426, art. 3, § 1, eff. June 14, 1973.

Now first of all we can disregard, as not relevant to the questions opened by this book, the purely *procedural* provisions of this Article, except to note that while the jury is held to "finding" on three "issues" only, "the court" (i.e., the judge) may admit in evidence "any matter" he "deems relevant to sentence"—a somewhat puzzling contradiction. (I should say once and for all, however, that intricacy of procedure, and even *purely procedural* "fairness," are no substitute for *standards* .) Let us rather concentrate on the three *issues* on which the jury must "find," listed in subsection (b) just above.

The first "issue," in subsection (b)(1), is really puzzling. Texas, in its Penal Code, defines "murder" as follows:

§ 19.02. Murder

(a) A person commits an offense if he:

(1) *intentionally or knowingly causes the death* of an individual;

(2) intends to cause serious bodily injury and commits an act clearly dangerous to human life that causes the death of an individual; or

(3) commits or attempts to commit a felony other than voluntary or involuntary manslaughter, and in the course of and in furtherance of the commission or attempt, or in immediate flight from the commission or attempt, he commits or attempts to commit an act clearly dangerous to human life that causes the death of an individual.

(b) An offense under this section is a felony of the first degree.

Amended by Acts 1973, 63rd Leg., p. 1123, ch. 426, art. 2 § l, eff. Jan. 1, 1974. [Emphasis added.]

"Capital murder," in turn, is defined as follows:

§ 19.03.   Capital Murder

(a) A person commits an offense *if he commits murder as defined under Section 19.02(a)(1)* of this code and:

(1) the person murders a peace officer or fireman who is acting in the lawful discharge of an official duty and who the person knows is a peace officer or fireman;

(2) the person intentionally commits the murder in the course of committing or attempting to commit kidnapping, burglary, robbery, aggravated rape, or arson;

(3) the person commits the murder for remuneration or the promise of remuneration or employs another to commit the murder for remuneration or the promise of remuneration;

(4) the person commits the murder while escaping or attempting to escape from a penal institution; or

(5) the person, while incarcerated in a penal institution, murders another who is employed in the operation of the penal institution.

(b) An offense under this section is a capital felony.

(c) If the jury does not find beyond a reasonable doubt that the defendant is guilty of an offense under this section, he may be convicted of murder or of any other lesser included offense.

Amended by Acts 1973, 63rd Leg., p. 1123, ch. 426, art. 2, § 1, eff. Jan. 1, 1974. [Emphasis added.]

Remember that this whole sentencing procedure applies only to persons *already found guilty* of "capital murder." Now since a "capital" murder, as § 19.03 (just quoted) says, must be a murder of the §19.02(a)(1) sort, where the defendant (see above) *"intentionally or knowingly"* causes the death (go back and check this if in doubt) then it seems certain that a jury, having found that the defendant "intentionally or knowingly" caused the death, *must already have found in the affirmative* on the *first* "sentencing" issue—the issue framed by Article 37.01(b)(1). Again, go back and check if in doubt. At the very best, the difference between "intentionally and knowingly" (§19.02(a)(1))on the one hand, and on the other "deliberately and with the reasonable expectation that the death . . . would result" (Article 37.071(b)(1)) cannot possibly be anything but totally puzzling to a jury, as it is to me, and as I am sure it is to you.

The *third* issue (Article 37.07(b)(3) above) is also quite puzzling. In the Texas Penal Code, "voluntary manslaughter," *not* a capital offense, is defined as follows:

§ 19.04. Voluntary Manslaughter

(a) A person commits an offense if he causes the death of an individual under circumstances that would constitute murder under Section 19.02 of this code, except that he caused the death under the immediate influence of *sudden passion arising from an adequate cause.*

(b) "Sudden passion" means passion directly caused by and arising out of provocation by the individual killed or another acting with the person killed which passion arises at the time of the offense and is not solely the result of former provocation.

(c) *"Adequate cause" means cause that would commonly produce a degree of anger, rage, resentment, or terror in a person of ordinary temper, sufficient to render the mind incapable of cool reflection.*

(d) An offense under this section is a felony of the second degree.

Amended by Acts 1973, 63rd Leg., p. 1123, ch. 426, art. 2, § 1, eff. Jan. 1, 1974. [Emphasis added.]

You can see right away, if you read the emphasized words in §19.04(c), that the jury, in deciding between "murder" and "manslaughter," and in rejecting "manslaughter" and finding the defendant guilty of "murder," has already as good as resolved in the affirmative this *third* death-penalty issue—the issue whether the conduct of the defendant in killing the deceased was an "unreasonable" "response" to "provocation" (Article 37.071 (b)(3) above). Here, again, the question of "reasonableness" of response and the question whether the "cause" of "sudden passion" was "adequate" are really the same question, or at least look so much like the same question that no jury could possibly tell the difference. Thus the *third* issue under Article 37.071(b) has, like the *first* issue thereunder, already been as good as resolved before the "sentencing" stage is reached, and the jury, as to these two issues, is called on only solemnly to repeat, in all practical effect, the findings it must have made already, when it found the defendant guilty of "capital murder" under Section 19.03.

This means that, after all, only the *second* of the three issues is actually of practical significance in fixing the life-or-death choice. Let me set it out again, to fill the cup of horror. The jury must decide:

"(2) whether there is a *probability* that the defendant would commit criminal acts of violence that would constitute a continuing threat to society;" [Emphasis added.]

People are then to live or die, in Texas, on a jury's *guess* as to their *future* conduct. (Incidentally, this is true whether or not my analysis of the other two "issues" is right, because a negative finding on the second issue precludes death—see Article 37.071(e)—whether the findings on the other issues be predetermined by the

"guilty" verdict, as I have argued, or are freshly made.)
This is really enough to stamp this section as outside the
bounds of civilized law. It seems almost supererogatory to
go further. But I must, for I want to cover the whole
ground. First, this guessing of Texas juries is to be in a
rather confined field; they are guessing *which people in
the narrow class of deliberate murderers* are likely to
commit the violent acts referred to, *in prison* or
elsewhere, many years later, if they are finally released.
Secondly, the named acts are described with double
vagueness. Hitting someone with your fist is a "criminal
act of violence"; does the section mean that a jury must
vote to electrocute persons shown to be given to fisticuffs?
If not, where is the line? Secondly, what is the difference
between "criminal acts of violence" which *do,* and those
which *do not,* "constitute a *continuing* threat to society"?
You may have an answer; I have none. But if you have an
answer, are you satisfied that an average Texas jury will
accept, understand, and follow it? Is this what they call a
standard in Texas? Not when I lived there; in those days,
they were more forthright.

Note, finally, that the jury, to support a death
sentence, must find "Yes," on each of the three "issues,"
"beyond a reasonable doubt." What on earth does it mean
to say that *"beyond a reasonable doubt"* a man will
"probably" be criminally violent? Can a jury handle a
crazy question like that? And does "a probability" mean
"some substantial chance" or "a better than even
chance"? Either usage is correct.

I picked up the statute from Texas because that
happens to be my home state; it was not selected as
conspicuously horrible. Obviously, we cannot analyze
them all. Bear with me (remembering the protruding
eyeballs) through one more of these new "standard"

statutes, again one which came to me at random, the one from Georgia. I reproduce it here from the Georgia Code, adding emphasis for clarity in the references to follow:

§ 27-2534.1 **Mitigating and aggravating circumstances; death penalty**—(a) The death penalty *may* be imposed for the offenses of aircraft hijacking or treason, in any case.

(b) In all cases of other offenses for which the death penalty may be authorized, the judge shall consider, or he shall include in his instructions to the jury for it to consider, any mitigating circumstances or aggravating circumstances otherwise authorized by law and any of the following statutory aggravating circumstances which may be supported by the evidence:

(1) The offense of murder, rape, armed robbery, or kidnapping was committed by a person with a prior record of conviction for a capital felony, or the offense of murder was committed by a person who has a *substantial* history of *serious* assaultive criminal convictions.

(2) The offense of murder, rape, armed robbery, or kidnapping was committed while the offender was engaged in the commission of another capital felony, *or aggravated battery*, or the offense of murder was committed while the offender was engaged in the commission of burglary or arson in the first degree.

(3) The offender by his act of murder, armed robbery, or kidnapping knowingly created a great risk of death to more than one person in a public place by means of a weapon or device which would normally be hazardous to the lives of more than one person.

(4) The offender committed the offense of murder for himself or another, for the purpose of receiving money or any other thing of monetary value.

(5) The murder of a judicial officer, former judicial officer, district attorney or solicitor or former district attorney or solicitor during or because of the exercise of his official duty.

(6) The offender caused or directed another to commit murder or committed murder as an agent or employee of another person.

(7) The offense of murder, rape, armed robbery, or kidnapping was *outrageously or wantonly vile, horrible or inhuman* in that it involved torture, *depravity of mind,* or an *aggravated battery* to the victim.

(8) The offense of murder was committed against any peace officer, corrections employee or fireman while engaged in the performance of his official duties.

(9) The offense of murder was committed by a person in, or who has escaped from, the lawful custody of a peace officer or place of lawful confinement.

(10) The murder was committed for the purpose of avoiding, interfering with, or preventing a lawful arrest or custody in a place of lawful confinement, of himself or another.

(c) The statutory instructions as determined by the trial judge to be warranted by the evidence shall be given in charge and in writing to the jury for its deliberation. The jury, *if its verdict be a recommendation of death,* shall designate in writing, signed by the foreman of the jury, the aggravating circumstance or circumstances which it found beyond a reasonable doubt. In non-jury cases the judge shall make such designation. Except in cases of treason or aircraft hijacking, unless at least one of the statutory aggravating circumstances enumerated in Code section 27-2534.1(b) is so found, the death penalty shall not be imposed.

One may note in passing that the death penalty *may* be imposed, apparently as a matter of sheer discretion still, for two crimes—treason and aircraft hijacking, a peculiar linkage, until one remembers who rides airplanes. In all other cases, what Georgia has done is to lay down a smokescreen of plenteous words, which, on hasty reading, mask the fact that exactly the same old unbridled jury discretion is there, if only the jury, guided by court and prosecutor, can grope its way through the verbal haze. For two things are clear.

First, a jury does not *have* to recommend death even if it finds one "aggravating circumstance," or many of these; besides, there is no review by anybody of a jury's *failure* or *refusal* to find an "aggravating circumstance" "beyond a reasonable doubt." Secondly, it is impossible to imagine a murder, rape, or kidnapping which cannot be described as "outrageously or wantonly vile" or evidencing "depravity of mind." How many rapes are not "wantonly vile" and "depraved"? *All* murder—the willful killing of a human being without justification or even adequate provocation—is "vile" and "depraved." Perhaps a few armed robbers might escape here as a matter of law, but how many could be sure of escaping under *all* of (3), (6), and (7)?

Look at (1). What do "substantial" and "serious" mean?

The best one can say is: (1) That the jury is in *all* cases entirely free, just as before the Furman case, *not* to recommend death, no matter what it "finds"; (2) that, on the other hand, except possibly for a few cases of armed robbery, and even fewer unimaginably abnormal other cases, the jury is in fact entirely free to *recommend* death, because kidnapping, murder, and rape *always* involve at least some "depravity of mind," and other such qualities set forth in the law; (3) the listed "aggravating circumstances" are in part (and every part is vital, for only *one* need be "found" to support a death sentence) exceedingly vague.

Note, moreover, that the *judge* may instruct the jury to consider *any* mitigating or aggravating circumstances which occurs to him.

(There is another feature, funny but for grimness, in the above Georgia statute, at (b)(7). Since Georgia law defines an "aggravated battery" as a battery (i.e., attack on the person) which deprives the victim of a member, or of the use of a member, or disfigures him, the concept is a preposterous one when applied to murder; either it is always present in murder, which deprives the victim of the use of all his members, or else it functions absurdly as an "aggravating circumstance," since it can make little difference to a dead man whether he can lift his right leg. I mention this inclusion of "aggravated battery" as an aggravating circumstance, supposedly present in some murders but not in others, as a symptom of the hasty thoughtlessness with which some of these new state statutes have been set into place.)

No jury need be hampered by such nonstandards. The practical position remains unchanged; the Georgia jury, without real restraint and without real standards, chooses life or death.

I am sorry for administering to you this dose of technicality. But had I not done so, I hardly think you would have taken my mere word for the real character of these new state statutes, purporting to set up "standards" for the jury's choice between life and death, in response to the 1972 Furman case's condemnation of standardless "discretion" in this matter. It is very hard to believe, until one analyzes closely, that the states actually have come up with such solutions in this most serious of matters. As it is, you will have to take my word, tentatively at least, that the statutes in other states resemble the two samples given; we cannot go through them all.

The facts of the matter are clear, nationwide and in the round. The new statutes *do not effectively restrict* the discretion of juries by any real standards. They never will. No society is going to kill everybody who meets certain preset verbal requirements, put on the statute books without awareness or coverage of the infinity of special factors the real world can produce.

And let us remember again that, loose and standard-less as they are, these new statutes would bridle discretion, if they bridled it at all, at only *one* stage in a process of choices. The decision what to charge, the readiness or nonreadiness to accept a guilty plea, the jury's selection of the offense for which to convict, the decision on "insanity," the decision on "clemency"—all these choices remain (to a degree totally unacceptable for the death-choice) without real standards, or highly vulnerable to mistake, or both.

Let us recall finally, here as elsewhere throughout the whole series of life-or-death decisions, the strange reciprocal relation between "vagueness" and "mistake." "Depravity of mind," one of the Georgia sentencing criteria, may seem to you, as it does to me, a term so vague as to make the "standard" in which it occurs a nonstandard, a pseudo-standard, a phrase having the look of a standard but possessed of no resolving power. But if another view be taken—the view that "depravity of mind" *has* a real meaning in some metaphysical sphere of transcendent lexicography, so that there is drawn, in that abstract realm, a real line between "depravity" and "nondepravity"—the position is still no better. For this precise meaning, even if assumed to exist, is not discoverable by humans. If there is a line, the light is too dim for us to see it. *Mistake* is therefore exceedingly likely—indeed, quite certain—to occur frequently. It really depends on our philosophy of language whether we say that this phrase, "depravity of mind," has no sharp meaning and so cannot decently be part of a "standard" or say that it *has* a "correct" meaning, so that every presented case does in fact fall on one side or the other of a line, but that this line (and this is the empiric fact, not changeable by philosophy) is impossible to locate accurately, so that mistake in judgment is certain. There is nothing to choose between these alternatives; neither will do for hanging men and women.

Chapter *8*

After Sentencing (Appeal, Post-Conviction Remedies, Clemency)

WE HAVE NOW brought the defendant through the entire first stage of the process of conviction and sentencing to death. We have seen that this process comprises either three or four main strategic choices—the choice of the prosecutor to charge a capital crime, the choice of the prosecutor not to accept a guilty plea to a lesser crime, the jury's finding of "guilty" on the capital charge, and (except as to the crime for which death is in some states the mandatory penalty) the sentencing choice, made by judge or, more commonly, jury, for death rather than for imprisonment. I think we have been able to see that, as to each of these choices, there is a far greater than negligible chance of mistake, and a quite unacceptable level of pure "discretion," without standards in law. This latter characteristic is found almost chemically pure in the first two stages—the prosecutor's decision to charge a capital crime and his decision not to accept a plea—and this fact alone is of crushing significance, for the plea-bargaining stage is the iceberg of which the rest of the criminal law is the tip that shows. In the two later stages we have covered—conviction and sentencing—we have seen that an exceedingly broad discretion, usually lodged in the jury, is masked by formal statements defining the "elements" of the crime, and by formal "standards" for sentencing; these definitions and standards contain terms of a vagueness entirely unacceptable in regard to the infliction of death, and they are in any case not actually binding on a jury that wants to show leniency—the other side of the coin being that any jury may use them as it will for the reverse of leniency.

This adds up to a system for making choices that we ought not to accept when the result may be death. But there is more yet. In this chapter, I shall carry the system on to the end.

First, of course, is the straight appeal. An automatic appeal is usually provided when the sentence is death— one of the many clear evidences, as saw in Chapter 4 above, of the recognition by our legal system of the uniqueness of death as a punishment. On this appeal, the higher court will consider whether errors in law have been committed.

Then there are other possible post-conviction remedies—*habeas corpus* and the like—a network of bewildering technicality, involving both state and federal courts, with the pattern varying for each state court system. It would serve no purpose for us to trace these out. Probably the most important thing to remember is that rarely does an appellate court, or any court in the whole post-conviction process, review as a new matter the "findings of fact" of the trial jury; I know of no case in which any such court has reviewed the prosecutor's choice to charge a capital crime or not to accept a plea; if such cases exist, they are so excessively rare that they make next to no difference in respect of the prosecutor's free discretion. Thus the whole appellate and post-conviction process exercises little corrective function over whatever mistake-proneness and standardlessness may flaw the process through trial and sentencing.

For the most part, these appellate and other post-conviction remedies have to do with *questions of law*. Also, the pursuing of these remedies requires resources—by which I mean money, for lawyers' fees and for other purposes. In the round, then, these judicial remedies after sentencing either share the weakness of the process up through sentencing, or suggest inquiry into the weakness analyzed in Chapter 9 (*Mistake of Law),* or are made partly or wholly inaccessible, or of greatly reduced efficacy, by the want of money, a problem general considered in Chapter 10. For these reasons, I shall not spend any more words on them, but ask you to keep them in mind when considering the matters raised in Chapters 9 and 10.

After all judicial remedies are exhausted, then we move into the stage of possible clemency. In the capital case, "clemency" means, almost invariably, the change of the sentence of death to a sentence of life imprisonment or of imprisonment for a long term of years; only in the rarest of cases, where clear proof of entire innocence comes to light between trial and execution, does any condemned man go free.

As to federal crimes, the power to commute death sentences is lodged by the Constitution in the President. In the states, the power is usually in the governor, but in some states boards either have the power or play some part in its exercise.

The clemency function in capital cases, like the prosecutor's function in deciding whether to charge a capital crime, or whether to accept a plea, is wholly discretionary, bound by no standards either published or discernible. A recent and most able short description of the process. Goldbarb and Singer, *After Conviction* (1973) on pages 343–348, makes this point repeatedly and unequivocally. *"While not exhaustive,* investigative reports in capital cases are *less perfunctory* than for other clemency applications"—a damnation with faint praise if ever I saw one. "While all states publicly announce the commutation decision, only a minority of the states publicly provide the reasons for their decisions." *"While it is impossible to know* which considerations are most influential when commutation of the death sentence is at stake, several obvious factors *probably influence* the decision." After this last sentence, Goldfarb and Singer mention intoxication, provocation, duress, viciousness of the crime, the degree of society's outrage, the fairness of the trial as perceived by the clemency authority, and doubts as to the guilt of the prisoner. This listing is not presented as exhaustive, nor do these factors stand in any fixed or statable relation to result; we have simply an open-end series of commonsense factors probably going into the making of a decision that is almost as purely discretionary as one's decision as to what college one is to attend.

One man has had his death sentence commuted because he "rehabilitated himself" while awaiting execution; others, equally "rehabilitated," die. Governors Alfred E. Smith and Herbert Lehman of New York, both great humanitarians, commuted the sentences of all those whose convictions the New York Court of Appeals had upheld by a *divided* vote. One survey seems to show that a positive recommendation of either the trial judge or the prosecuting attorney—a recommendation altogether discretionary and bound by no standards—is exceedingly important. There is some indication that favorable publicity has an effect; this is indeed almost a corollary of the factor, mentioned above, of the degree of societal outrage.

Some governors who wholly disbelieve in capital punishment have commuted all death sentences. Others of the same opinion consider it their duty to leave some scope of operation to the state's law on the subject, regardless of their own beliefs, and commute selectively. Former Governor Michael V. DiSalle of Ohio, a man whose humaneness shines in his book, *The Power of Life or Death* (1965), seems to have been of the latter sort and, in the book, gives us what is probably the fullest record we have of commutation philosophy as held by a single man who has wielded this terrible power. What appears is, indeed, a most admirable use of discretion—"clemency" at its best—but the book is on the other hand a thorough documentation of the lack, in the clemency process, of anything that could possibly be thought to approach a standard, and a documentation, as well, of the entire dependence of the quality of "clemency" judgments on the personality of the official empowered.

In Connecticut, we are told by Goldfarb and Singer, it has been the practice to schedule the commutation hearing early on the day set for execution, and to require the attendance of the doomed man. I suppose that if the decision were for death, some reasons might be given, perhaps even on the spot. But those reasons could never be reasons rooted in law. For clemency knows no standards that are invocable as a matter of law. To the saved, this is mercy, of a quality not strained. To those who learn they are to die, it is irrational choice for death—the final such choice in a long series. From that point on, there is no discretion; the human race becomes a killing-machine.

Chapter 9

Mistake or Uncertainty of Law

So FAR I have dealt, at every stage, with the problems of mistake on questions of fact, and with the problem of vagueness or near-meaninglessness in the "standard" for some finding—say, the finding of "not guilty by reason of insanity," or the finding of "premeditation." The picture cannot be rounded out without some attention to still another matter, one of very great difficulty—the problem which may (depending on one's legal philosophy) be thought of as the problem of "mistake of law," or the problem of "uncertainty of law."

"Questions of law" have been looked on, classically, as questions concerning the correct *rule* to apply to facts assumed to be known; this concept has eroded in modern time, but it will still do for a first approximation. Now in the course of criminal proceedings an enormous number of *questions of law* may be decided. Was the search of the defendant's home lawful? If it was not, is it the correct rule that the evidence found must be excluded at the trial? Has the defendant a right to the assistance of counsel, paid for by the state, from the moment of arrest? May the defendant's pastor be forced to testify as to a confession made to him by the defendant? Is a prospective juror who expresses distaste for the death penalty to be dismissed? Is it unlawful for the trial judge to express or indicate his own opinion of the credibility of an "alibi" witness? Does the defendant's ninety-day period to appeal include July 4? Does the evidence support a verdict of "guilty" of "felony murder"?

Hundreds of such questions of law, great and trivial, may be raised and answered in the course of a criminal proceeding, from arrest until the final appeal in the last post-conviction proceeding. Some are obvious of answer. Some are sufficiently difficult that learned judges will disagree on them. Not only the Supreme Court of the United States but the Supreme Courts of the states may and often do divide very closely on such questions, great and small. Yet the answer to the question of law, in a capital case, may decide the issue of life or death for the defendant.

Under an older and today much weakened view of the nature of law, each such question had a "right" and a "wrong" answer; the "right law" was somehow *there,* to be discovered or found by the correct use of technical reasoning. Among some lawyers and among some other people, this is still the prevalent view—more often assumed than expressed. If it is the correct view, then the workings of the capital punishment system are connected in a simple way with the decision of questions of law. Because if there exists a correct answer to every legal

question then it is perfectly plain that *mistake* is possible
and must sometimes occur, just exactly as mistake is
possible, and must sometimes occur, with respect to the
numberless questions of *fact* which have to be decided as
a person is moved along the line from freedom to
execution. No one could think that courts are infallible
on points of law, or believe that there are not many
questions of law—including many life-and-death questions—the answer to which, even if a "correct" answer
exists, is exceedingly elusive and hard to be sure of. If we
had no other way of knowing this, the close votes on
courts of last resort—often five to four in the national
Supreme Court—would irresistibly convince us of it. (It
was noted in Chapter 8 that, for just this reason, some
governors have commuted *all* death sentences affirmed
by a divided appellate court.) There probably is a "right"
answer to the question whether there is life on Mars, but if
nine equally well-accredited astronomers divided five to
four on the answer, we would know with absolute
sureness that the right answer was hard to find or to be
confident of. (And we must not forget that there was a
time when nine astronomers out of nine would have
opined that the sun went around the earth.)

On this view—the older, perhaps classic view—of
law, we are—just as in the case of doubtful questions of
fact—executing people as a result, sometimes, of flatly
mistaken determinations of law. The alternative hypothe-
sis is judicial infallibility—even five to four or four to three
infallibility—and no sane person has ever claimed
infallibility for any institution except the Papacy, and that
only under the most rigid rules and on the most
infrequent occasions, and on the basis of an assumption
of divine guidance, hardly an assumption that fits our
judges.

A newer and now quite prevalent philosophy of law changes and complicates—but in no way improves—the picture. Close questions of law, under this view, have no single ."correct" answer; there is no law out there somewhere, waiting to be seen clearly. The situation is, rather, that judges, using the technical resources available to them—mainly precedents, statutes, and constitutional provisions—strive for law which is not disobedient to these, and which to some extent is channeled by these. But they often find that these authoritative materials do not settle, and cannot by any logical manipulations be made to settle, the question before the court. (This, in a nutshell, is because *words*, whether in statute or constitution, do not have fixed meanings through their whole range, and because no *precedent* is ever exactly like the case at bar—to which may be added the fact that American courts are not and never have been bound to follow every precedent every time, but have always had and exercised the power occasionally to *overrule* a precedent, though the occasions on which this may properly be done are themselves not susceptible of precise definition.)

This newer philosophy of law goes on to say that, where the technical materials (precedents, statutes, constitution) do not produce a clear answer—a condition often evidenced by disagreement as to the answer among equally competent and disinterested people—then obviously, since an answer is given, *something else* produces it. This something else may be the judge's sense of policy, justice, fairness. This is undoubtedly the usual case, in overwhelming preponderance. The judge may, in obedience to the style of our law, conceal the operation of these factors from the public or, quite often, from himself, but they must be there, or disagreement on questions of law among equally learned and honest judges could not occur. Competent mathematicians do not divide five to four on a question about the topological properties of a Moebius strip; if they did (and sometimes they do so divide, for a time only, on very new questions) we others could only say, sensibly, that the answer is not yet known.

Let me give an example. In the 1940's, a man named Willie Francis was condemned to death by electrocution. He was strapped in the chair and the current was turned on, but there was a malfunction and, while he could feel the current, it did not kill or seriously hurt him. He was unstrapped and taken back to his cell, to await repair of the apparatus. There was no showing of any *intent* on the part of the state (Louisiana) authorities to inflict any needless suffering. (Willie was seventeen.)

A *habeas corpus* (see Chapter 8 above) was quickly taken out, on the proffered ground that a *second* electrocution, or attempt at electrocution, would, in co-action with the first, add up to a "cruel and un- usual punishment," within the ban of the national Constitution. This question of law reached the Supreme Court, which decided, five to four, that the Constitution was not violated. The next time, the chair worked.

Now there were good arguments here on both sides. One would have to start—as so very often—with the concession by all hands that the ratifiers of the invoked constitutional provision had no "intent" whatever, positive or negative, about this. Is an *accidentally* "cruel" punishment within the ban, particularly where the avoidance of it (by canceling the second execution attempt) is easily possible? Or is a state held only to doing its best to avoid cruelty in administration of punishment? And so on.

The view of the nature of law prevalent in modern

times would say that there is no "correct" answer, discoverable by sound technical manipulation of given authorities. And this seems very plain, in the very case, and in a veritable host of other cases.

Yet people die, as Willie Francis died, on the basis of the courts' answering such questions as though they did have a "correct" answer.

At best—and, as I have indicated above, this is usually the case—what this really means is that, in the innumerable zones of genuine doubt as to "right" law, judges' view of policy (not necessarily expressed) form the decision. In this process there is inevitably, as every serious student knows, room for working of the personal value preferences of the judge. (Lest I be misunderstood, let me say at once that of course no judge in the Francis case liked double electrocution; the preferences were partly of an institutional kind, and had in part to do with general attitudes toward the broad or narrow interpretation of constitutional guarantees.)

As to questions of law, then, we have to sum up about like this: If the older view of law as a fixed and preexisting body of rules is correct, then *mistake* is plainly possible, and in view of the very great difficulty of "finding" this law—a difficulty irrefutably proven by chronic division of opinion, on issue after issue, among competent and honest lawyers and judges— *mistake* is likely to be of frequent occurrence. If, on the other hand, the newer philosophy of law is right, and many "close" questions really have no answer discoverable by technical means, then decision is being made by the operation of judges' views (to a great extent undisclosed) on policy and fairness—with frequent divisions of opinion, among equally informed and intelligent professionals, as to where good policy and fairness are to be found.

This is the system we *have* to use for legal decision; it

is bootless, therefore, to ask whether it is good enough for the decision of ordinary cases. But, as we have seen in Chapter 4, the fact that a system is good enough, or has to be accepted as good enough, for ordinary decision does not imply that it is good enough for the choice between life and death. I submit that our intellectual apparatus for making decisions on close questions of law—whether you accept the old model of law that is certain but hard to find, or the new model of law that is continually being created by whatever enlightenment the judges may possess for the time being, shaped in the large, but not compelled, by antecedent authority—I submit that this system, not of our choice but the consequence of our built-in limitations, *is not good enough* for choosing people to suffer or not to suffer a bitter and cruel death. I haven't any idea how we could make it good enough; that is not my task, for I would be against capital punishment even if judges were endowed with some unimaginable infallibility as to decisions of law.

I will close this chapter by mentioning one exceedingly disturbing aspect of the "mistake-of-law" or "uncertainty-of-law" problem. There is continual *change* in the nature of what is accepted as correct law; as I have pointed out, American courts can and do overrule their own precedents. The last seventy-five years, for example, have seen a continual shift toward our judges' finding, in the Constitution, more and more stringent guarantees of defendant's rights, and this change has been participated in by all or virtually all the Justices of our Supreme Court, though by some more whole-heartedly than by others. State courts, too, change on their holdings as to definitions of certain crimes, standards of evidence, and so on. (Of course I am not here referring to *legislative* change, but to fresh and altered perceptions of courts, without legislative intervention.)

The inevitable result (a mere obvious corollary of the uncontroverted fact of change) is that some people have in the past been convicted of crime, although, either as a matter of substance or as a matter of procedure, the law has changed so as to make improper, today, convictions obtained on the same facts or by the same procedures as those previously approved.

This raises the celebrated problem of *retroactivity*. Should a man who is in prison as a result of a 1943 trial, in which he was denied state-paid counsel, be released, or tried again, now that the Supreme Court has held counsel must be provided? Should a man convicted in 1954 on evidence not now admissible be released? Should a man now be freed who was sent to prison on the basis of a definition of the word "accessory" now rejected by the state Supreme Court?

There is no good *general* solution to this retroactivity problem, either doctrinally or practically, and I am not going to attempt one here. My point here is that, where the original proceedings were *wrong enough,* under presently accepted standards, to call for release or new trial, this is *possible* in cases of imprisonment and does sometimes occur.

There is an exceedingly interesting variation. Sometimes the former trial went wrong—badly wrong—not because a question of law was wrongly decided but because the question itself was not yet fully visible, even to lawyers. I believe the Sam Sheppard case is an instance of this. Sheppard was tried, in the early 'fifties, for the murder of his wife. His trial was conducted as a circus, with the judge as ringmaster, and with the nation's lines of mass communication locked on the sensational aspects of the story that unfolded. This, incredibly but truly, was more or less the normal way of running murder trials in those days, whenever other sensational news ran short. Sheppard was convicted of second-degree murder (obviously a compromise verdict, for the state's whole case was such as to make it first-degree murder or nothing). He went to prison. In the succeeding years, there slowly began to develop a body of judicial doctrine setting bounds on the sensationalism of murder trials. After some twelve years in prison, in this quite altered climate of opinion and doctrine, Sheppard was released by *habeas corpus,* on the ground, obviously right, that the sensational publicity surrounding his trial had made his trial unfair.

Now I don't care whether you think that a great deal of "retroactivity" of this sort is good. Hardly any reasonable person can deny that some of it is good. The clear, flagrant, and plainly harmful error of law, resulting in severe punishment, ought at least in the worst cases to be corrected, just as the plain error of crucial fact can be and ought to be corrected, however belatedly.

And the point here is, of course, that the error of law, like the error of fact, is uncorrectable, however urgently it may call for correction, after the execution of the defendant. The doctors have buried their mistake. If Sam Sheppard had been hanged, then we would have had to live morally without any possibility of undoing the work of a clearly disgraceful trial.

Mistake of law, then, can occur—or law is in close cases uncertain. One of these things is true, or both are true. When made as a result of the resolution of a genuinely close question of law, then, the choice for death runs a great risk of being either mistaken or arbitrary and standardless. This plain fact must be added to all the others, of similar form, that make our legal system not good enough to choose people to die.

Chapter 10

The Warping Effects of Race and Poverty

THERE WERE, at the last count available to me, 114 persons under sentence of death in the United States. Of these, 61, substantially more than half, were black; three were American Indians. No statistics are available to me that show it, but anyone at all familiar with the subject would know that all or almost all of the 114 are poor, at least in the frame of reference wherein the expenses of effectual defense against crime are to be calculated.

What does poverty mean when set against the background of the system of choices for life or death, described in the preceding chapters?

Most capital offenses are unbailable, or bail is set so high as to be absolutely inaccessible to any but the affluent. This means that in the capital case every kind of activity outside the jail—the marshaling of testimony, the verification of facts—must be carried on by somebody other than the defendant. This means money. If I were charged with murder, and if my defense (which I myself knew to be true) were that the deceased had threatened to kill me with a knife (as in the Arizona case mentioned in Chapter 6), I would want a thorough professional investigation conducted into the habits of the deceased with respect to carrying and threatening to use knives. I would want my own people looking into the question whether a knife had been found in the vicinity, and into whatever traces might exist—such as, say, the story of a hardware-store clerk—that connected that knife with the deceased. I would want to find out as much as I could about his prior record of arrests for violent crimes, of psychiatric confinement, and so on. I would want to have located and interviewed all possible witnesses to his demeanor and words just prior to our private meeting. *Above all, I would want a lawyer—not an overworked "public defender," not "assigned counsel," but the best criminal lawyer in town,* to advise me, and to work with the detective agency employed by me, toward providing everything we needed for the best possible defense case. Are not these the very minimum requirements of prudence?

But all this costs money—lots of money. So does everything else I am about to describe. I think I could just barely raise enough money for something like a fairly adequate defense—though this would utterly ruin me (and would utterly ruin most of my readers if they were in this position) because adequate investigation and good legal counsel come very, very high. But it is all completely out of the reach of the poor. The poor man—unless some public-interest organization happens to see an important issue in his case—can no more afford a really adequate defense than he can afford a year's cruise around the world on a luxury liner. He may luck out, one way or another. But he will be very heavily handicapped from the beginning.

Now this (even at this early stage) readily transposes into the key of possible, and increasingly probable, error; if a defense cannot be presented in the best possible manner, the chances of even a valid defense's being rejected are obviously increased. To the defendant, the finding of that knife may mean the difference between life and death; to the rest of us, the defendant's not finding it may mean that the court and jury, acting for us as a society, will overrule a self-defense plea that was actually valid, and sentence to death the wrong man—a kind of moral death for all of us. But we are not ready to furnish poor defendants with really adequate resources for the development of a defense, by investigation at early stages while the trail is still warm. Even if we were, the resources in manpower do not exist. We are running a system, therefore, which from the very beginning—from the hours and days following arrest—so operates as to make it enormously more difficult for the poor to bring out all the truth than it is for the well-to-do to bring out all the truth. This is, of course, just another way of saying that both conviction and conviction by mistake are from the beginning made much more likely for the poor.

Let us pass on to plea-bargaining—the point at which most criminal cases are settled, the point at which, in possibly capital cases, the decision is made by the prosecutor whether to accept a plea of guilty to a noncapital offense or to press on, with the maximum charge, for death. One of the most careful studies I have seen of plea-bargaining, that in Donald Newman's *Conviction* (Little, Brown, 1966, pages 215–217) comes down very hard on the importance of having skillful counsel at this stage, a stage which Newman says ". . . requires no less *skillful* legal ability to evaluate alternatives than is required for other decisions where evidence and convictability are involved" [emphasis added]. I have emphasized the word "skillful" because I want to stress, yet again, that at this stage you need not just any lawyer, any overworked assistant public defender or assigned counsel, but a *skillful* lawyer, skilled in this very specialized matter, and able to give it his time and undistracted attention. To get him, you have to pay for him, and pay plenty. He is not ordinarily available to the poor. So, again, the fact of poverty makes it quite plainly more likely that, in general, the indigent will have a much slimmer chance than the well-to-do at this exceedingly significant point, where the prosecutor, by deciding whether to accept a "plea," is making the choice between life and the possibility—from this point on a substantial possibility—of death.

On to the trial. It is almost supererogatory to point out at what a disadvantage the poor person stands when this stage is reached. Part of this disadvantage has to do, again, with the *investigation* vital to development of the case. I have already alluded to this at an earlier stage, and need only add that this handicap is compounded and increased when one reaches the showdown stage of trial, where all the evidence must at last be produced if it is to have any effect. *The development of an evidentiary case costs money;* the state does not, to any adequate extent, if at all, furnish that money. Another part (and what a vital part!) of the poor man's disadvantage has to do with the *quality* of his legal representation. Good trial lawyers—skilled cross-examiners, gifted advocates—are now charging something not far from $1,000 per day of trial. But if we are (as we certainly are) committed to using an *adversary* system to get at the truth, and if we base this adversary system squarely on the energy and skill of lawyers, how can it possibly be that it makes no difference whether you have a superb lawyer or a mediocre lawyer? Nobody really believes this; we just prefer to shut our eyes to the obvious fact that the poor man, in a capital case as in other cases, is at a crushing disadvantage—a fact which, from our standpoint as well as his, carries the inevitable (but morally shocking) implication that his execution through mistake of fact, or by the application of "discretion," or by the jury's misunderstanding of some cloudy concept like "premeditation" or "insanity," is more likely than it is for the well-to-do person, who can (by ruining himself, at least) bring it about that his case be put to judge and jury in the most favorable light by a lawyer talented and skilled in just that art.

The appeal stage (including all post-conviction proceedings and motions) is more of the same. At this point, what is needed is lawyers' skill in researching and arguing questions of law, and above all in *spotting* these questions. Here again, who could be so naive as to think that it makes no difference in the result whether a superbly gifted advocate is employed (at the high price he commands) or, on the other hand, one has the services of a conscientious but not superbly talented assigned counsel or public defender? But if this difference *can* make a difference in result, then obviously, once again, the poor are at a heavy disadvantage.

The 1963 Supreme Court case of Gideon v. Wainwright, holding that poor people must be provided with counsel at state expense, may have had the unfortunate side-effect of lulling us to sleep on this issue; the disadvantage of the poor remains, for what is needed is not just *any* lawyer, but a lawyer specialized and highly skilled in criminal defense. Volunteer and assigned counsel, like "public defenders," often (though not always) do a good job, but you and I know perfectly well that what we would want would be the best criminal lawyer procurable. Gideon v. Wainwright does not guarantee any particular quality of representation.

(I ought to add that lawyers' skill in spotting and arguing questions of law is also important at the *trial* stage; I have known of criminal cases which were irretrievably lost, not because there was no error of law in the trial, but because the defendant's lawyer failed to make timely objection to such error.)

Obviously, the very same points can be made as to the "sentencing" stage in some of the new statutes discussed above in Chapter 7. The *discovery and proof* of "mitigating" circumstances, and the *rebuttal* of evidence of "aggravating" circumstances, may require costly investigation. The placing of these circumstances before the jury in the most favorable light to the defendant calls for advocacy in a high range—both as to talent and as to fee.

Now we come, at last, to the stage of clemency. Insofar as the sentence-commuting authority (governor or board) tries to base its decision on some fairly definite grounds, it is again obvious that the proper presentation of these grounds, from the defendant's side, depends on investigation and advocacy of a high—and costly—order. Even the effective invocation of "discretion" is an art at which not all are equally skilled.

Now stop and consider. Can you really doubt that a process like this, from first to last, is *heavily* loaded against the poor? Could you really be surprised at finding that by far the majority of people suffering death are poor? Are you satisfied with that? If you are not, face the fact that there is no way to change it except to do away with the death penalty; our society is never going to support fully adequate defenses, all the way up, for the poor, and even if it would there are not enough first-class lawyers to go around; the situation would be like the one suggested when, in an old movie, a character ran for the Senate on a platform including the promise that every American boy was to have an education in Harvard College.

Let me now correct one possible misapprehension. I have not said, and do not believe, that affluent people *improperly* or *corruptly* escape capital punishment. What I have said is that they, unlike many of the poor, can have developed, and brought before the appropriate authories, material that may bring about decision in their favor.

Now what about blackness? Why are more than half of the people on death row black in a country with about eleven percent blacks?

A great deal of the explanation is contained in what has already been written in this chapter. There is a high correlation between blackness and poverty. But I must, to be candid, open up another possibility—one which must remain no more than that but which must be taken seriously. The system I have sketched, in Chapters 5 through 8, is riddled and saturated with uncontrolled discretion, however disguised. I am not sure we can yet assume, after the history of three hundred years, that this "discretion" may not be influenced (often, to be sure, unconsciously) by race.

I will not insist on this. What I will insist on, as a matter of common knowledge, is that where standardless "discretion" plays a part, or where close decisions of fact must be made on disputed evidence, or where vague and ambiguous concepts ("premeditation," "insanity") must be applied to concrete facts, we are one and all susceptible to the tendency to see things in a better or worse light depending on our general sympathies; we fight against this, but in the end only the self-deluding think they can wholly avoid it. If this idea is right, then there is the ever-present danger that anyone against whom, for any reason, conscious or unconscious prejudice exists will come off worse than a person against whom such feeling does not exist. And of course the *unconscious* prejudice, the prejudice one thinks one has wholly overcome, is the more dangerous.

In any case, most people on death row are black, and almost all are poor. What is *your* explanation? And can you go on living with such a system?

(I ought to remind you, again, that all these considerations apply to all infliction of punishment. I cannot think that any of us can be satisfied with this condition or cease from efforts to better it. But at the very least such a system should not be employed to select some people for the supreme agony of execution. I have already shown in Chapter 4, that by ceasing to use the system for this end we are not committing ourselves to abandoning criminal punishment altogether; in law, as in life, death is supremely different.)

Chapter 11

A Summary—
Law New and Old

Now I HAVE SKETCHED a shocking picture. I know that I have not meant to mislead, and I think I have not misled; minor mistakes could hardly affect this crushing case. I will not now recapitulate in detail, but will remind you only that the decisions on charging, on acceptance of guilty plea, on determination of the offense for which conviction is warranted, on sentencing, and on clemency add up (for somewhat different reasons in each case, discussed in the chapters above) to a process containing too much chance for mistake and too much standardless "discretion" for it to be decent for us to use it any longer as a means of choosing for death. We have to keep using it as a means of choosing for other punishment, even as we slowly try to make it better, but for the death of a person it will not do, and it cannot be reformed enough to do.

Suppose all the mistake-proneness and standardlessness I have laid out, step by step, were concentrated in the decision of one man. We would regard that as so evidently intolerable as to be undiscussable. But it might be better than what we have, for responsibility would at least be fixed. All our system does is to diffuse this same responsibility nearly to the point of its elimination, so that each participant in this long process, though perhaps knowing his own conclusions to be uncertain and inadequately based on lawful standards, can comfort himself with the thought, altogether false and vain, that the lack has been made up, or will be made up, somewhere else.

How have we allowed ourselves to get here? I suggest it is because of our seeing the whole process through the medium of a radically false mythology. We tend, I believe, to think of persons' being "clearly guilty" of crimes for which they ought to die. Then some of them, by acts of pure grace, are spared—by prosecutors' discretion, by jury leniency, by clemency. After all, who can complain at not receiving a pure favor? (There is here perhaps a touch of Calvinism—but to a true Calvinist a blasphemous touch, for the "grace" comes from humans all too human.)

The trouble is that the system may just as well be viewed, and with enormously higher accuracy, if numbers count, must be viewed, as one in which a few people are selected, without adequately shown or structured reason for their being selected, to die. The inevitable corollary of sparing some people through mere grace or favor is standardless condemnation of others. The thing that ought to impress us is the standardless condemnation; we have been looking too long at its mirror image; we should take courage and turn around.

One paragraph corrective of a possible misapprehension: When I condemn our capital punishment system as intolerably mistake-prone and standardless, I do not mean in any way to suggest corruptness or cruelty on the part of those who work it. The prosecutor *must* accept some pleas and reject others; I have no reason to think that most prosecutors do not try to exercise this function in a commonsense and humane manner. Juries *must* pronounce on the questions put them; if they are asked whether a particular murderer or rapist was "depraved" or "not depraved," they have to answer as best they can; if they are given an unintelligible "sanity" question to answer, they must do their best. Judges must pronounce on questions of law, whatever they may know as to their own fallibility. I have already given illustrations of the humane use of the clemency power by governors. All this is not to say, of course, that there are not some hanging prosecutors, hanging juries, hanging judges, and hanging governors. But, overwhelmingly, the trouble is not in the people but in the system—or nonsystem.

Now I have not bothered you with constitutional law. All the arguments I have put forward, without a single exception, would support the abolition of the death penalty even if there were no Constitution of the United States. But lawyers among my readers will readily see that, all the while, I have been arguing a Fourteenth Amendment case too; I have argued that there is not enough "due process of *law*" in our system to make it an acceptable instrument for the "deprivation of life." And I have here emphasized the word *law* because it is the most important word in the phrase. Good *procedure* is not enough; the bedrock guarantee is that nothing will be done to anyone without an adequate *law* that commands it—a law, I think I am warranted in saying, whose required clarity is a function of the gravity of the thing being done, as I have argued at length in Chapter 4 above.

I have not so clearly argued an Eighth Amendment case, condemning the death penalty as "cruel and unusual." But I think such a case is implied in what I have said. Probably an accurate partial gloss on "unusual" would be "not of regular or predictable incidence." And I should think the psychological cruelty of death by the human killing-machine would be greatly heightened by the victim's awareness—not from reading this book but from knowing what crimes were committed by people playing ball out there in the exercise yard—that he has been chosen without solid reason in law for the difference in treatment.

But this book is for the laity, and I quickly retire from the constitutional arena. I will close with a story about a development in the law of another time and place.

The Law of Moses is full of the death penalty. But as time went on the court in ancient Jerusalem, without of course touching one syllable of this Law, devised *procedural* safeguards so refined, so difficult of satisfying, that the penalty of death could only very rarely be exacted. So approved was this process that it is said in the Talmud that when one rabbi called "destructive" a Sanhedrin that imposed one death sentence in seven years, another said, "Once in seventy years," and two others said that, had they been on that great Court, *no* death sentence would ever have been carried out.

Now I used to think, superficially, that what this story meant was that the ancient Jews, abhorring the infliction of death, seized on a purely collateral and accidental means—complication of procedural safeguards—to avoid its infliction, just as the English judges of about 1800, administering capital punishment for some 250 crimes, became terribly fussy about the exact wording of indictments. And I thought the quoted remark of the two rabbis merely expressed dissatisfaction with that lack of ingenuity which had resulted in some cases' slipping through the procedural net.

As I have looked at our own system for administering capital punishment, and as I contemplate the entire insufficiency of its remotely possible improvements, I think I see a different and infinitely profounder point in the story. At this level of profundity, "procedure" and "substance" lock and become one.

I think the rabbis, in surrounding the punishment of death with nearly unsatisfiable *procedural* safeguards, were groping (or perhaps consciously moving) toward a truth reached by the quoted remark of the two last mentioned. To put it in terms they might naturally have used, I think they were saying at last, "Though the justice of God may indeed ordain that some should die, the justice of man is altogether and always insufficient for saying who these may be."

I suppose, really, that is what this book has been about.